Uncle Bill's Tin Hat

MICHAEL ANDREWS and VINTY MURPHY

First Published 2015.

Copyright © 2015 Michael Andrews and Vinty Murphy.

The moral right of Michael Andrews and Vinty Murphy to be identified as the joint authors of the work in all jurisdictions has been asserted by them. The right of Michael Andrews and Vinty Murphy to be identified as the joint authors of the work has been asserted by them in accordance with the Copyright, Design and Patents Act, 1988.

All rights reserved. No part of this publication may be reproduced, stored in a retrieval system or transmitted in any form or by any means, electronic, mechanical, photocopying, recording or otherwise, without the prior written permission of the authors or as expressly permitted by law, or under the terms agreed with the appropriate reprographics rights organisation.

Enquiries concerning the reproduction outside the scope of the above should be sent to the publisher at the address below.

You may not circulate this book in any other binding or cover and you must impose this same condition on any other acquirer.

ISBN NUMBER: 978-0-9933905-0-0

Every reasonable effort has been made by the authors and the publisher to trace the copyright holders of material in this book. Any errors or omissions should be notified in writing to the publisher, who will endeavour to rectify the situation for any reprints and future editions.

Design: Liam O'Connor.
Editor: Deirdre O'Neill.
Print: Walsh Colour Print.
Publisher: Michael Andrews and Vinty Murphy.
             Merrion Road,
             Dublin 4,
             Ireland.

DEDICATION:

This book is dedicated to those who fell. From the Somme to the Dardanelles, from Ypres to Kut-al-Amara, or any of the dreadful battlefields of World War I, they are left behind in graveyards stretching over whole hillsides, far from home.

It was remarkable to see at the National Library's open day when Bill's Tin Hat was archived, how few of those attending were direct descendants of the soldiers who had left the mementoes: they were nephews, cousins, grand-nephews and friends rather than sons or grandsons. This was because so few had returned to marry and have normal lives and families after the war.

Bill Andrews showed courage and durability on the battlefield but of far greater significance was his good luck to survive the random carnage of the trenches. It is the most disgraceful aspect of World War I that young lives were squandered with such reckless disregard by those entrusted to lead them.

This book is dedicated to those who didn't come home.

CONTENTS

CHAPTER		PAGE
1	Born in Gaol	1
2	Boy to Man	15
3	To War	25
4	Out of the Trenches	39
5	Mespot	61
6	The Family Man	81
7	World War II	99
8	The Time of his Life	127

Preface

This helmet ("tin hat" to the soldiers), dating from the World War I Battle of the Somme, was long a private curiosity in the extended family of Bill Andrews, known as Lieutenant William Andrews to his wartime companions and to his grandchildren as Uncle Bill. His was the head that the helmet protected when it collected its dramatic damage. It emerged into the public spotlight only as its hundredth birthday approached. In 2013 the National Library invited holders of World War I memorabilia in the Dublin area to bring them to the Library to be photographed and recorded. Cameras from the TV stations appeared in the waiting room and the helmet caught the reporters' eyes.

That was not surprising; there can be few examples of a war memento as immediately evocative of the terror experienced by men at the front line. The damage to its steel vividly illustrates the devastating power of shrapnel. A fragment has ripped through the helmet's steel. Without further explanation, the viewer knows the terrible damage that it would inflict on human flesh. The astonishing survival of the young Irish officer who was wearing it, and the presence there at the Library of his son and grandson, completed its attraction. We were gratified by the intensity of the welcome and the publicity this familiar family memento received.

Bill was an Irishman through and through despite his name, his near fifty years living in England and his two world wars in the British Army.

On leaving the National Library that day, it occurred to us that we should record the story of the helmet and the genial young Irish engineer officer who wore it.

This book is the result.

Chapter 1

Born in Gaol

BILL'S HELMET.

This is Bill Andrews' helmet which saved his life at the Somme in World War I, one of the bloodiest battles in history. It was struck in hostile fire only once, on the night of the 10th July 1916 at the village of Contalmaison. It was created to protect a soldier's head and it did just that: Bill Andrews was struck in the head by a spinning shard of shrapnel. The helmet took the blow and received a savage-looking gash but served its purpose, protecting Bill from injury or death. The dramatic gash reduced the helmet, in his fellow-soldiers' eyes, to just another piece of battlefield detritus to be cast aside. Bill disagreed.

Uncle Bill's Tin Hat

Very few damaged helmets have survived to be preserved for us today, a century later, for a very good reason: they were of no use on a military battlefield and were thrown away as debris or melted down for reuse as shells or bullets.

The circumstances that saved the helmet were told by Bill himself: he was knocked unconscious by the blow but he woke up on a stretcher. The helmet was about to be tossed away to the side of the trench. "Give that here to me," he said, "It saved my life," and they placed it on his chest as he was stretchered away.

We have sought out the story behind the helmet, when and how it was created and the circumstances that led to its protecting Bill Andrews' head. We have also tried to discover the story of the life it saved, Bill's childhood and adulthood, his strong but fun-loving character, the events in his life that led to this point of impact and, most important of all, what he did with the rest of his life, the extra 45 years won for him by the helmet.

Were it not for this helmet, neither of the authors of this book would exist, for Bill was only a young man in 1916: his wife and children came later and they included Michael, the co-writer of this book, and Joan, mother of Vinty Murphy, the other co-author.

This is the story of the helmet and the life it saved.

Bill Andrews liked to make a memorable entrance and his first was no exception, taking place as it did within the cold stone walls of Omagh Gaol. His parents lived in one of the wardens' stone houses in the prison. In June 1892 Mary Ellen, his mother, was once again heavily pregnant and about to give birth to her seventh child. She was American-born but she had close relatives living in the country near Omagh and she was expected to go to a relative's home for the delivery. She preferred the comfort of their living quarters in the prison and so she gave birth to Bill in the bedroom of the warden's house and another wailing voice was added to the cacophony of prison.

Mary had been born in Philadelphia, the daughter of a porter. Her parents named her Ellen: how she came to be known as Mary we do not know. She had met up with Bill's father, William, when he most needed her skills as a teacher. He had been raised on a tiny 4-acre farm in County Meath and was an illiterate road-worker when they met. Soon after, he was spotted as an able young man and offered a job in the prison service on the one condition that he first learn to read and write. Luckily, Mary was at hand and she set about coaching him.

THE STRULE RIVER IN OMAGH WITH THE GAOL IN THE BACKGROUND.

As soon as he gained the secure job in the Queen's service, they were married. She bore and raised their brood of children (with the help of an aunt of hers, Anne, who became the family housekeeper) and at the same time built up her own career as a schoolmistress, running a small school in Killyclogher, outside Omagh.

Each day she put on her hat, climbed into her horse-and-trap and drove right through the town and out the country road to the school. This made her quite the exception as a wife of a prison official, combining a profession with the raising of a large family. She was even known to stop off in the Campsie Bar en route home in the afternoon and partake of whiskey in the upstairs parlour with the owner, Peter McAleer, while his wife tended bar downstairs. The lives of the McAleer and Andrews families were to become entwined with each other for the whole of the 20th century.

So, as well as being born in gaol, Bill went to school from a home inside the prison walls. He passed through the gaol arch every day to get to and from school, a terrifying dark space for a young boy, where the inner gates banged shut behind him, locking him in the black archway to be scrutinised by the turnkey before the outer gates opened, letting him run out into the light and on up Castle Place and Abbey Street to his classes in the Christian Brothers' School.

Bill's father had great success in his work, his innate skills and his

THE GATEWAY TO OMAGH GAOL.

THE OCTAGONAL GOVERNOR'S HOUSE, SITED AT THE CENTRE OF THE GAOL WITH WINDOWS OVERLOOKING EACH OF THE PRISON YARDS.

sensitivity to both his colleagues and his charges helping him all the way up the promotion ladder from the bottom rung. By 1900 he was living in the governor's house at the centre of the gaol, although his title was only deputy governor. This house is still standing by the Strule River as a stumpy octagonal tower in the centre of the compound, its windows and balconies overlooking the many courtyards and lockups where the prisoners lived. There were two gates adjacent to the front door of the house, one leading to the prisoners' cells and the other to the walled garden around the house, which was an oasis of peace with its own fruit trees, flowers and vegetables.

Across the courtyard was the treadmill building in which there was a tread wheel for punishing inmates with hard labour. They had to walk the tread wheel, turning it with their legs like hamsters in a cage, to pump water up to tanks on the roof for the gaol water supply.

It was in this building that executions by hanging had taken place, but the last of these was carried out in 1880. Thomas Hartley Montgomery was one of the last to be hanged – for hacking to death his friend, the bank cashier William Glass and then proceeding to rob the same bank. Montgomery was a police inspector and took charge of investigating his own crime. It was only when his gambling debts came to light and his superiors had him scrutinised that he was found out. On the night of his hanging a great storm broke over Omagh, which was taken as a sign that a deceitful evildoer was receiving justice.

OMAGH GAOL. THE GOVERNOR'S HOUSE IS THE OCTAGONAL BUILDING AND THE TREADMILL BUILDING IS ON THE RIGHT.

The wardens' living conditions were comfortable, with gas and electricity and a good stove in the basement. The Andrews couple had respectability and a steady income. Despite both father and son being named William, the name of King Billy, the Protestants' champion of 1690 and the Battle of the Boyne, the Andrews family were Catholic and Mary's school was attached to the parish chapel at Killyclogher. To some of their fellow-Catholics they were traitors who had taken the Queen's shilling and given up fighting the invader. To others they were just managing to winkle some money out of a government which had a history of anti-Catholic discrimination; better a good income should go to one of "us" than one of "them".

Bill was the youngest boy in the family and his elder brothers, John and Michael, were teenagers when he was only eight. His sisters, Bee and Nell, were aged 11 and 10 and there were two younger sisters, Mary aged 6 and Kitty aged 3. Bill was thus the only boy amidst a clatter of girls and he had to develop his independent and resilient nature to hold his own in the family as well as at school.

OMAGH TOWN 1901.

Much of this information comes from the census of 1901. Mary Ellen and Aunt Annie pulled the wool over the census-taker's eyes by lying about their ages, knocking several years off the real figures. It is just as well that these census returns remained confidential for 100 years, keeping them free from suspicion. Only historical research has revealed their deception.

The existence of two family tragedies is contained in the cold archived statistics of the 1901 census. There had been another son. He was born in 1889, three years before Bill, and christened Frank, but he died of burns in a fire at the house at only 17 months. The tragic event can only be discerned from his death certificate, which gives the cause as "Burn – 2 Days

BILL IN 1904 WITH HIS SISTERS, BEE AND MARY.

Exhaustion". Open fires, candles and oil lamps were an essential part of life in every house, each a continuous source of fire hazard, and it is not surprising that many young children died in household accidents.

Bill had another sister, Annie, then aged fifteen, but her name does not appear on the census form because she was not in the family house on the night of the 31st of March. She was delicate and spent long periods away in the country recuperating from bouts of illness. She too was never to reach full adulthood, finally succumbing when she was twenty.

The wars of Bill's youth were the Boer wars in South Africa and he could not escape hearing all about them. Nationalist Ireland supported the Boers as an oppressed minority rebelling against the British Empire, but Bill's father was in the pay of the British authorities and the family home was tied to his job so loyalties were divided. Many Irish volunteered for service in the British Army against the Boers and others volunteered on the Boer side: these were treated by the British authorities as traitors and, if taken prisoner, were shot as spies rather than corralled as prisoners of war.

The iconic helmet of the Boer wars was the white pith helmet of the British soldier, originating in India and made from the compressed fibres of the Sola, an Indian swamp plant. It was designed for protection from the tropical sun rather than enemy bullets, with a high vented crown and long

front peak and neck guard. These proved disastrous in southern Africa: their deep neck guards made it impossible to shoot from the prone position and the troops had to raise themselves on one knee to fire. Conspicuous white helmets gave the skilled bush marksmen of the Boer armies perfect targets. They were able to pick out helmeted soldiers at up to a mile distance. The troops covered their helmets in sand-coloured sacking to camouflage them or just wore cloth caps.

Uncle Bill's Tin Hat

We know little about Bill in his growing years. We know that he was a good student. One of his school-mates became a Christian Brother and taught one of Bill's sons. His comparisons in class favoured the father over the son. We know Bill felt some lack of affection, as he himself said, long after, that he thought his mother "never really liked him". Belonging to a large, relaxed family of sisters and brothers was at least part-source of his gregarious nature, natural interest in the lives of others, his sociability and considerable charm.

His father, with whom he lived after the closure of Omagh Gaol and his move to Cork without Mary Ellen to become Governor of the Women's Gaol, does not seem to have been a typical prison governor. He was remembered as a man of some gravitas, but there was never mention of harshness, cruelty or arrogance.

Comfortable in his own skin, he expected to receive due regard from others – and to return it. What we know about him, three counts: first, his inexorable rise through the service (not by any means an inevitable career pattern for someone from his far-from-affluent background); second, that he was given charge of women prisoners both in Omagh and again in

CORK CITY GAOL.

Cork; third, that he and the family found it quite natural for him to bring three young children with him to Cork and take sole care of them – he didn't bring Aunt Anne to help. These all give a picture of a relaxed figure, confident, capable and well balanced. The one or two letters of his that have been preserved are in very finished handwriting and carefully composed; their content is to do with family matters rather than news of his own doings.

Old William and Mary Ellen were a close couple who overcame obstacles and tragedies and were painstaking over every aspect of their large family's upbringing, notably education. Although, in later years, their individual career paths caused them to be physically separated, their bond remained strong. From that unshakeable unity their children gained enough strength and self-confidence to take on the wild upheavals of the world they emerged into.

At the other end of Omagh town in the house where Mary Ellen had been known to sip whiskey brought up from the bar, a bright young girl was growing up. She was Christina, the second of two sisters born in the same year, 1896, to Johanna, the second wife of Peter McAleer.

Peter was a businessman who had been granted a bar licence and expanded the business to become general merchant, goods importer and travel agent. His first marriage was a tragic instance of the dreadful scourge of tuberculosis. He was happily married to his first wife Mary and she became mother to five young babies before the disease struck each one in turn. One by one they died and were buried in the little graveyard in Killyclogher. Then Mary herself caught the consumption and there was nothing that could save her. Her name is the last on that side of the gravestone, closing a tragic chapter on Peter's life.

At thirty-eight years of age Peter found himself a widower with just an aching void to show for his years of being married, five pregnancies, five births and six graves. He was tough, physically and mentally, a trait associated with the Northern Irish. He continued to manage his businesses unbowed. The story goes that, on a visit to the house of another prosperous Catholic family, the Laffertys, during the evening two young ladies, cousins of his hosts, sat at the piano to play a duet. The fire's warmth and the soft music and the candlelight on the two intense young faces melted the heart of the hard-bitten businessman. One of the ladies was Johanna and she soon accepted his proposal and became his wife. They had many children and lived together to ripe old age.

Uncle Bill's Tin Hat

It isn't always just sweet music and mellow whiskey when you take on the run of a bar in Omagh. The McAleers were still the innkeepers of the Campsie Bar in the 1970s and 1980s when Northern Ireland was targeted by bombers. Three times the bar was bombed. The first time a "ten minutes to get out" warning was shouted in the door and, sure enough, the bar and house were both demolished in the blast. They were rebuilt straight away – it's said that some of the same men rebuilt it as planted the bomb – and when the second bomb was planted some time later it caused considerable damage but the new building resisted the blast better.

CHRISTINA AND KATHLEEN MCALEER PHOTOGRAPHED IN 1897.

The third time, one of the regulars, tired of having his drinking disrupted, tied a rope around the device and dragged it outside and off down the road to a ditch where the explosion caused little or no damage at all.

The big bomb that is synonymous with the name Omagh was set off on a Saturday afternoon in the late 1990s, when the peace process was well advanced and coming to a successful outcome, ending the years of maimings and killings. It was planted only two hundred metres or so up the main street and caused appalling loss of life, killing twenty-nine people and unborn twins and injuring countless others. This time the only damage to the Campsie Bar was to have its windows shattered.

Johanna's second child was born, in the same year as her first, 1896, on Christmas Eve, and, because of the date, was called Christina. She grew up in Omagh and was educated in the Loreto Convent, still extant. As she

THE CAMPSIE BAR, 1903. PETER AND JOHANNA MCALEER, CHRISTINA'S MOTHER AND FATHER, ARE AT THE DOOR ON THE LEFT, WHICH IS THE ENTRANCE TO THE FAMILY RESIDENCE.

was leaving school in 1915 the Imperial Civil Service, realising that their pool of exclusively male entrants was being scooped up by the armed forces, began to seek ladies to join the service. They set up a programme of competitive examinations nationwide, the nearest to Omagh being held in Belfast. The nuns packed their prize pupil, Christina, off to try her hand. She comfortably exceeded the cut-off mark and was offered a job in the Savings Bank in London where she settled.

Many years later in that city, she met a dashing young man from her home town. He had a charismatic reputation for bravery in the war and a dented old helmet under his bed. His name was Bill Andrews.

Chapter 2

Boy to Man

It was William seniors' promotion that led to the greatest upheaval in Bill's young life, the move to Cork with his father and two sisters while his mother stayed on in Omagh with three daughters and her housekeeper aunt, to run her little school in Killyclogher.

HIGH STREET, OMAGH – THE COURT HOUSE IS AT THE TOP OF THE STREET WITH THE CHURCH OF IRELAND STEEPLE BEHIND IT AND THE TWO ASYMMETRICAL STEEPLES OF THE CATHOLOIC CHURCH TO THE RIGHT.

For a Victorian Era couple, Bill's parents were surprisingly modern and took this separation in their stride. They had shown themselves to be ambitious and upwardly mobile, Mary Ellen giving William the educational start to his career and then persevering with her own school project. William senior had risen from being a prison warden – who could have grown to despise his inmates – to Deputy Governor, yet one of the few opinions passed down from him was that he wanted to see the women's prison in Cork shut down. He seems to have specialised in women's prisons and there is a strong family belief that he was pleased to see the women's section of Omagh Gaol closed in 1903. He saw that it was doing no good for its inmates and how inappropriate it was for them to be locked up for "crimes" they had committed out of need or inability to cope.

CORK CITY GAOL.

Cork women's prison had room for 300 inmates, with about 20 female staff – nurses, teachers, wardens, cooks and domestic servants. There was one maintenance man employed there who, along with Bill and his father, made up the entire male complement among about 350 women. This must have been an extraordinary place for a teenage boy to grow up. William senior had enough confidence placed in him to be entrusted with the upbringing of his son and two daughters in this inelegant setting.

Bill was by no means a lily-white schoolboy. One of the few stories he recounted of his boyhood was an occasion when he was serving Sunday Mass in the parish church and found that he had a marble in his pocket. Of course it had to come out and be pushed around on the top step as he knelt in front of the altar, reciting by rote the Latin responses. One push too far and the marble ran away from him and rolled to the edge of the top stone step and then, infinitely slowly, tipped over and bounced noisily on each step before tapping to a halt at the altar rail. The congregation held its breath and the deep silence only exaggerated the noisy clack of every bounce. Then everyone pretended nothing had happened until Bill was later read the riot act by his father, an experience he never forgot.

At about this time Bill's two older brothers achieved independence and left home. John, the eldest, joined the postal service and worked in Kilkenny, where he rose to the position of postmaster. Michael, next in line and eight years Bill's senior, completed a degree in civil engineering within a year or two of their move to Cork and, as soon as he was qualified, left for England to gain experience. He joined the Board of Works in London and stayed there for the rest of his life. He married an English girl and they brought up one son, Raymond, a distinguished architect in later life.

Mary Ellen was a working wife, not in the least unusual today, but rare in those days. She kept on her work as a primary mistress while giving birth to no less than nine children. Of course that meant that a housekeeper was needed and a Victorian problem provided the solution:

THE GOVERNOR'S OFFICE IN CORK CITY GAOL.

unmarried ladies were numerous and had little chance of employment. Her unmarried aunt Anne became the family's housekeeper. In Omagh, Mary Ellen established a new household in a rented house with three of her daughters and Aunt Anne. She, like her husband, had to leave behind the orderly life within the Gaol and set up her own household in the town.

Just a few months after its division, tragedy once more visited the family. Their eldest daughter, Annie, now working in the post office in Omagh, became seriously ill yet again. She had always been delicate. William senior hurried back from Cork. When he arrived, all there was to be done was to say his farewell and be at her side as she faded away. Her death certificate records that he was present at her deathbed just as he had been at her little brother Frank's twenty years before. There followed her funeral, a second family parting and the sad journey back to Cork to resume the responsibilities of looking after a large prison and three growing children.

Bill, in later years, was a leader and a confident taskmaster to both his army subordinates and his growing family, with a natural sense of authority. His time with his father in Cork is the likely source of these traits – William senior was also in a position of authority and expected those in his care to live up to his set of rules. He was used to having Mary Ellen beside him and was now without her in a new city with a new challenge, dealing with the prison in its entirety, staff problems, housekeeping, security and maintenance as well as its function as a penal institution. He had to use his time effectively. The likelihood is that, as young Bill grew towards adulthood, his became the ear his father confided in. He had the opportunity to observe the work of a successful manager dealing with problems and keeping things running smoothly. His confidence and his trust that he could sort things out came naturally from this tutelage.

As in Omagh, Bill went to the Christian Brothers College in Cork City. He did well there and gained a place in University College Cork to read for a degree in civil engineering.

The move from school to university brought a huge and totally welcome change from the rigid regime of the Christian Brothers. He embraced his new freedoms with delight. Superficially the change was minimal: he still lived at home and walked to lectures as he had walked to school, but the increased scope and liberty of university life meant a lot to him. He did not abuse this freedom by neglecting his studies – a civil engineering degree is a tough grind – and he qualified on schedule.

> *Queen's College Cork was founded in 1845 under charter from Queen Victoria along with two similar colleges in Belfast and Galway. They were created to allow for the education of all religious denominations, as Catholics did not generally attend Trinity College Dublin although there were no legal restrictions preventing them. The three colleges together made*
>
>
>
> UNIVERSITY COLLEGE CORK.
>
> *up the Queen's University of Ireland which later (in 1880) became the Royal University of Ireland.*
>
> *In a strange precursor of partition, the Belfast college was separated out from the others in 1908 and became Queen's University Belfast, while the other two became colleges in the federated National University of Ireland system.*

Bill would have preferred to study medicine (his ideal was to be a children's specialist) but was told that there simply wasn't enough money for that. His college years he always remembered with pleasure and told tales about his lectures and exams, whereas he never spoke about his schooling.

At his final exams he had a viva voce session before a small exam committee. He was asked the definition of "work" and answered correctly that it was the product of the force applied and the distance through which it was exerted. "Suppose you hold a twenty pound weight off the ground with your arm extended from your body – holding it still. Are you performing work?"

"No. I'm exerting a force but that force does not move through any distance."

"Yes, correct. Now, can you explain why your arm gets tired?"

Bill couldn't explain it. Forty years later when his son was in turn taking his final exam in civil engineering, he recounted the question to him, adding that he thought it an unfair one to put to an undergraduate. He wasn't holding a grudge, just still trying to work out what would have been the intelligent answer.

THE ANDREWS FAMILY IN CORK, 1912: WILLIAM SENIOR AND BILL AT THE BACK, NELL, MARY-ELLEN AND KITTY IN THE MIDDLE AND BEE AND MARY IN FRONT.

The daughters in the family were not, apparently, considered for university education. Mary, Bill's sister, later in her life after their parents' deaths, took a degree in medicine – she'd seen Bill's disappointment at missing out on this career. Those girls developed a high opinion of their proper social status and their potential upward mobility. That was a natural carry-over from their parents' successful rise in the world, best seen in William senior, who was born into a large family eking out a living from a tiny four-acre holding, barely educated, married to the daughter of a porter, and yet three of his children felt it quite natural to take university degrees.

The daughters made up their minds that their parents' progress should continue through another generation. Matrimony, rather than assiduously laboured-at careers, was their preferred choice for this purpose except for Mary who never married – not even once – and relied upon her medical vocation. In this endeavour for social progress the sisters succeeded admirably and to an extent that is quite surprising to record. All three who married became prosperous, even wealthy, personalities in Dublin's social life. Although they married four men in total, these men seldom appeared. They departed to heaven or to England and they left their widows/ex-wives well off. One sister managed two marriages – her first husband left her a widow with two children, her second departed to the Other Island before following the first to eternity. He had added only one further child to the family.

Another's spouse left her a childless widow, and a very wealthy one, to the extent that her home in later years was in a fashionable hotel from which, well dined, she is reported to have sallied forth daily in her car. It was her good fortune that the roads of her time were much less trafficked than now and that another thirty years would go by before the invention of the breathalyser.

As late as the millennium year, one of Bill's grandchildren, a newly appointed partner in a substantial Dublin firm of solicitors, was asked by the firm's Grand Old Man if he had any connection to "those Andrews sisters", remembered as big names about town in their heyday.

The history of helmets is as long as the history of war itself, but in 1910 to 1913 they were for ceremonial purposes only. They were the beacons of horse-borne officers, plumed and glinting in the sun for their men to follow. Bill had seen pictures of the ultimate show of helmeted horsemen at the

THE FUNERAL OF KING EDWARD VII, 1910.

funeral of King Edward VII on 20th May 1910. The kings and emperors of Europe were there in their military finery, all related to each other through their common ancestry, mostly through Queen Victoria, and they included the new British King, George V, Kaiser Wilhelm of Germany, King Alfonso XIII of Spain, King Frederick VIII of Denmark, King Haakon VII of Norway, King Ferdinand of Bulgaria, King Manuel of Portugal, King George I of Greece and King Albert I of Belgium. Their helmets of silver and gold, plumed with ostrich and peacock feathers, glinted in the Windsor sun: all were to become embroiled in the coming war – on both sides.

Bill graduated in 1913. Political conflict was, in this year, coming to a head: in Ireland the Republican camps were vying with each other as to whether to seek total independence or a form of home rule, the Unionists were arming and agitating to stay within the United Kingdom and workers were demanding better pay and conditions than the miserly employers were prepared to give.

A certain Vladimir Ilyich Lenin was preaching communism from central Europe.

All these developments were heedlessly ignored by government. The states of Europe, more concerned with the jealousies among their heads of state, kings and emperors, tsars and archdukes, were embroiled in their own rivalries over their conquests in Africa and beyond.

Boy to Man

From University College Cork Student Register for First Years 1910-1911

William Andrews

Academic Year	1910-11
Class Year	First Year
Surname	Andrews
Christian Name	William Paul
Age	18
Place of Birth	Omagh
Place of Education	Christian Schools, Omagh
Religious	Catholic
Name of Father	William Andrews
Parents' Residence	HM Prison, Sunday's Well
Name of Guardian	T.E. Weekes
Matriculation	NUI Senior Grade Intermediate 1910

He graduated with a BE in 1913

BILL'S ENTRY IN UNIVERSITY COLLEGE CORK STUDENT REGISTER.

It was also a time of great social innovation. The state old-age-pension was introduced for the first time in Britain. The cinema had been invented and cars were seen on the streets. Bill had many social events available to him, no doubt including girls and parties. Yet as soon as he graduated in 1913 he left for England to gain employment and a salary and to experience the joys of his youth. Like all of his generation he was blithely unaware that these joys and this youth and his whole generation were about to be blown apart by war.

Chapter 3

To War

We know little of what Bill did in England in those early days except from his own descriptions of how a young engineer was paid little and had to earn respect and adapt to tough working conditions on building sites. He had one self-deprecating tale in which the young engineer was being taken on for the duration of a building job and the employer had to settle his pay. The boss asks, "What are we paying labourers these days?"

THE SUFFRAGETTE MOVEMENT.

"Seven quid a week" is the answer. "OK," to the graduate engineer, "Seven quid a week it is."

He started out in London, the London of the suffragettes, labour unrest and political reform. The suffragettes were a thorn in the side of authority, and were persistently arrested and jailed, then went on hunger strike and were force-fed to prevent the uproar their deaths would cause. In June 1913, just as Bill took his first steps in London life, Emily Wilding Davidson decided to publicise their demands by throwing herself in front of the king's horse at the Derby. She died of her injuries and the suffragettes were suddenly the new political force.

Bill saw growing labour unrest and workers' protests against inhuman housing and working conditions. In Dublin that summer, the police forcibly broke up a trade union protest in Sackville Street, killing one worker in the mêlée. Then two tenement buildings in Church Street collapsed, killing seven residents. An outbreak of general rioting followed and the trade unions came out in strike. The great lockout of 1913 followed, Jim Larkin its leader, which was the baptism of fire for the unions in Ireland.

But Bill was enjoying life. He somehow obtained employment, poorly paid and lasting only as long as each particular building project. He lived in digs in London, Liverpool and Edinburgh. He was free and life was good. He moved around England and ended up working for Edinburgh Corporation in Scotland in 1914.

This year was still a time of optimism and social tension until the great powers suddenly tipped the world into war. They had been vying with each other over colonial conquests in Africa and the division of spoils from the decline of the Ottoman Empire. The small emerging nations of eastern Europe saw this as their opportunity for freedom from the ancient empires. One small blow for this freedom was the assassination of the heir to the Austrian throne, Archduke Franz-Ferdinand. The powers had woven a delicate web of mutual-assistance alliances around themselves and they were quickly ensnared in its tightening strands. Austria-Hungary and Germany mobilised their massive armies. Germany

THE BOILING POINT.
PUNCH CARTOON SHOWING WORLD LEADERS, THE KAISER IN THE MIDDLE WEARING HIS PICKELHAUB HELMET.

To War

BILL'S FAMILY WITHOUT HIM, 1914: TOP: MICHAEL, MARY ELLEN, WILLIAM SENIOR AND JOHN O'DRISCOLL, NELL'S HUSBAND. FRONT: KITTY, LIAM AND NELL WITH BABY MOIRA. LIAM AND MOIRA ARE THE CHILDREN OF JOHN ANDREWS, BILL'S BROTHER.

invaded Belgium: Britain and France came to Belgium's aid and Russia declared against the central powers.

Suddenly a summer of holidays and festivities was overturned by declarations of war, patriotic propaganda, calls to save the empire, to stop the rape of the small nations, to tame the German bear.

> *By 1914 the armaments industries, especially in Germany and France, had made great improvements in artillery guns and ammunition. The German high command was the first to appreciate their significance and invested heavily in new artillery and had rejigged tactics to match, with meticulous arrangements for keeping the artillery supplied throughout their first precipitous advance. As a result the German army started with a clear advantage, which led to its sweeping early victories.*

The 77 FeldKanone 96n/a shown was one of the workhorses of the German artillery; 5,086 of them were manufactured. The barrel diameter is 77mm (about 3 inches). It commonly fired a shell that was time-fused and contained both shrapnel and high explosive at an effective range of 5,000m and, as with all artillery manufactured since 1897, it was recoilless.

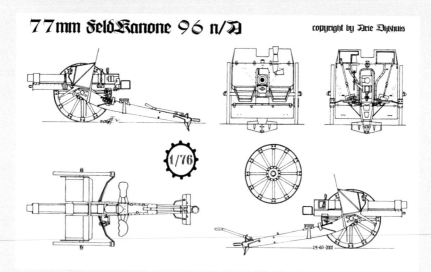

That taming of "recoil" revolutionised the rate at which guns could fire. A device to absorb the recoil of an artillery piece was fitted to a French gun produced in 1897 and that device transformed its effectiveness. Before this invention, each time a gun was fired the recoil was violent enough to lift it off the ground and throw it backwards. This was awkward and potentially dangerous for the gunners, but a greater effect on the gun's rate of fire was that this movement completely disrupted the gun's "aim". Re-setting the gun then took several minutes. Once the recoil's effect had been tamed, the gun's setting was no longer disturbed each time it was fired which enabled the firing rate to rise dramatically, to ten times faster or more. All the big powers had to copy this immediately and they all possessed recoilless artillery by the start of World War I.

At first the war was one of movement. The Germans swung through Belgium with measured disregard for its neutrality. The French had withdrawn their forces 10 kilometers from the frontier as the deadline approached so that they could not be accused of having provoked an invasion. They need not have worried. Their allies had no doubt as to who the aggressor was.

Belgium resisted as best it could, King Leopold leading his country in what they knew was futile military resistance but gaining the respect of his nation and the onlooking world in the process. The Germans took the southern towns of Belgium and wheeled into France. The British expeditionary force came to the aid of the French army, but even together they were not able to stop the might of the Prussian military machine.

The Germans were within 15 kilometers of Paris when they were confronted by a cobbled-together French army which had been rushed in Paris taxi-cabs from the streets of the capital. At the same time the Germans ran out of supplies and ammunition and had to bed down for a few days. The French and British armies dug in to positions in front of them and quickly built up their defences. Trench warfare had begun. It was not yet Christmas of 1914 and the soldiers on both sides, who had been promised a victorious return to their families for Yuletide, were now confronted with impassable mud and barbed wire between them and the enemy.

Overnight the rules of war were turned on their head. Instead of rushing across open country led by officers on horseback, the troops were hidden below the fireline, under the flailing metal from exploding shells and the bullets from snipers and machine guns. Instead of rallying regimental flags and bugle calls, concealment and silence were necessary to prevent attracting a barrage of shellfire. To attack meant to throw hundreds of your own men into the crossfire hell of no-man's-land in the hope that some of them might reach the enemy trenches, there to use grenades and bayonets in hand-to-hand fighting with the entrenched enemy. If they won out they dug in again and hoped for reinforcements before the enemy regrouped. The officers of the higher command were in tents behind the lines, working out shelling patterns and supply logistics and pushing raw recruits around the map to plug the holes in the lines.

The need for steel helmets arose from the same improvements in artillery guns that gave the Germans their initial advantage. The rifle and the machine gun were the iconic weapons of World War I, but shrapnel was its most deadly killer. Any helmet using steel light enough to be worn in

THE FRENCH ADRIAN HELMET.

battle would be easily penetrated by machine-gun or rifle bullets. "Rifling" in those guns' barrels gave the bullet a spin which meant that it could be given a penetrating shape – the spin keeping the point facing forwards – and this combination of spin, pointed shape and supersonic speed gave a rifle bullet formidable penetrating power.

Early in the war the French realised that shrapnel, unlike rifle bullets, could be deflected by a helmet. Shrapnel reached its victims with deadly speed certainly, but did not have the surgical penetration of the rifle bullet. The French developed the Adrian helmet, with a deeply rounded shape and a narrow peak and a neck guard, designed by August-Louis Adrian. It was churned out in millions as the war continued. Its success in the field led the British to consider a similar helmet for their troops. For some reason the French Adrian helmet became the favourite of the Russian and eastern European armies and the version with a large red star insignia became the iconic symbol of the Soviet soldier.

The man who undertook the British design was John L. Brodie. The *appearance of the helmet was not his foremost consideration. His design had a shallow steel crown and a wide brim. This shape could be machine-pressed in one piece, which simplified manufacture of the vast quantities required. Critically, it provided excellent protection from shrapnel. It was quickly put into mass production.*

SOVIET VERSION OF THE ADRIAN HELMET.

The first to be delivered to the trenches were kept as "trench stores" in the front line, to be used as the need arose. It was only in the summer of 1915, when over a million helmets had been manufactured, that they were issued for general use. By March 1916 they had reduced head injuries by 75 per cent.

BILL'S BRODIE HELMET.

The static war ground on throughout the winter into 1915. Enlistment in the army became the duty of every young man with aspirations to manhood. Soldiers in uniform were the stars of the day. Rallies were held to encourage enlisting, employers sent whole companies of their employees to sign up. Only the conscientious objectors and the Irish Nationalists voiced their opposition to recruitment, the latter urging their supporters to fight for Irish independence instead. They were vehemently decried in the press for this treachery and their public rallies were violently broken up.

RECRUITMENT POSTER.

To War

ANTI-RECRUITMENT POSTER.

Bill was well aware of this Irish response to the British enlistment campaign. Into 1915 he was working in Edinburgh for the City Corporation: this was a relatively good job for a young engineer although it would still end in his being let go as soon as the current construction work was finished. Nevertheless, it showed that he was making his way on the ladder of employment. In Scotland there was a strong Irish presence and the differences between Irish Nationalists and their Unionist rivals were well understood and caused many violent confrontations. Bill was not left untouched by these forces. The decision he had to make was whether to sign up for the British Army, as was expected of him and as so many were doing all around him. The footballers of Hearts of Midlothian Football Club in Edinburgh signed up en masse, leaving their team to be rebuilt from the amateur ranks.

Uncle Bill's Tin Hat

Workers on the grand estates and in factories were formed into "buddy" companies and sent to France with their lorded employers as their officers. This was the most important decision of Bill's life. He had an available escape route, back to Ireland where he could at least find some form of employment and where compulsory conscription was never applied for fear of the opposition it would arouse. He had enough of an education and innate realism to see through the propaganda and the public fervour. To join up meant to expose himself to risk of death and complicity in the deaths of others, and yet it was the popular option, embracing the surge of public sentiment, following the path taken by his mates.

But it was his choice to make and he never shirked from a decision. It meant a rejection of the nationalist fervour that was sweeping his own country, Ireland, and an acceptance of the "taking the King's shilling" mark of opprobrium. He seems to have acted instinctively rather than with deep thought or balanced motives, following his desire for

NEWLY COMMISSIONED BILL IN HIS OFFICER'S UNIFORM, 1915.

adventure. His decision made, he signed up as a volunteer. Even though he survived – with the help of the helmet – the scars of this war were to stay with him throughout his life and eventually cut short that life. He never regretted his decision to sign up, even when he was gasping through the lung disease that the trenches gave him. Early on he met a returning Irish regular army soldier in London and he asked him what it was like to fight in the trenches. The man said it was indescribable, so bad that you were only living from minute to minute trying to survive. The soldier taught him his survival technique, St. Patrick's Breastplate, a prayer he had learnt as a child and which he recited to himself when he needed its protection. Bill learnt it and used it in the same manner:

Christ as a light illumine and guide me,
Christ as a shield o'ershadow and cover me,
Christ be under me, Christ be over me,
Christ be beside me on left and on right,
Christ be before me, behind me, around me,
Christ this day be within and without me. Amen.

This is the version of the prayer that he learnt and used to fortify his defences in the trenches and until the day he died. He also passed it on to his children. There are many other versions, but this one has the benefit of brevity which is paramount on the battlefield.

When Bill joined the army he was issued with a uniform, an officer's cloth cap and a horse. No helmet. He himself provided the other necessary component, his sense of humour – modifying his strong ego – and it was needed in his early steps in military life, which he recounted in later days as complete comedy. Having a degree from university (a much rarer qualification then than now), he was immediately designated for a commission and was asked which regiment he would prefer from a list of alternatives given to him. Knowing little of the British Army, his eye was caught by something with an Irish flavour and so he found himself being interviewed for a commission in the Irish Guards. Little did he know that the officer corps of any Guards regiment, especially the Irish Guards, is drawn exclusively from the aristocracy and consists almost entirely of ex-pupils of the English public school system. Bill reported for interview at an imposing regimental headquarters where the interviewing committee

Uncle Bill's Tin Hat

had only one question of any importance: which school did he come from. Their expectation was somewhat dented when instead of Eton, Harrow or Marlborough, he replied, "Christian Brothers, Cork."

Given a second choice of regiment after this debacle, and perhaps slightly better informed, he lighted on the Royal Engineers, commonly called the Sappers, which was not a Historic Regiment. It had been founded during the recent Boer wars for construction – called civil engineering – in the battlefield milieu. Bill had plenty of officer qualities and was accepted. He found, once settled in, that military life suited his personality, and his service in the army was eminently successful.

There were two separate courses for officers, a general one for all officer cadets and the second more particular to each man's specialisation, in his case the Sappers. The general training included horsemanship and, feeling somewhat apprehensive, he prepared for this by taking lessons at a riding school. He was taught the finer points of Parade Ground Deportment: right hand free and resting on the pommel; left, holding the reins, to be maintained four inches above the horse's neck and six inches from the rider's body. Armed with these tips, although really quite inexperienced, he bestrode his mount with such military poise that he caught the eye of his instructor on the first day and was selected out to join the "advanced" instruction group.

THE WARHORSE ON PARADE.

First he had to pass a preliminary test. The group was mounted in a long row, side by side, each facing a jump. On the order, "Cross stirrups. Drop reins. Fold arms," and then "Forward on the command and take the jump before you," they were all expected to clear the jump as if riding bareback. He recalled tumbling off at, or possibly before, the jump. He gracefully accepted relegation back to the main class. The relevance – or irrelevance – of this training to the frontline trenches in France, his first posting, is self-evident.

THE HORSE AT WAR, WEARING HIS GAS-MASK. HIS HANDLER IS WEARING HIS OWN GAS-MASK AND A BRODIE HELMET.

In fact there was some justification for this form of training as he did use his equestrianism in his later posting in Mesopotamia, where horseback was an essential form of personal transport.

"Improvisation is the essence of the art of military engineering" was a phrase he would come out with from time to time, mostly on the rare occasions when he attempted odd jobs around the house. He first heard it at his officers' training course for the Sappers, and it's the only word of that course that he ever passed on to his children. He made improvisation his metier: coping, wangling, making the best of what was available, and he thrived in his role as a young officer in the Royal Engineers.

Training over, on 25th November 1915 he embarked to join the British Expeditionary Force in France and to be initiated into the world of the Sappers in the fields of war. He joined his first Company at Armentières in Belgium and it was soon in the field behind the frontline trenches.

He had visited the town one evening and arrived back quite late. On his way through the camp he came upon a fracas. A soldier from his unit was at the centre of it. Wild drunk, he was holding a group of NCOs at bay by whirling his rifle around his head at the end of its lanyard. They had tried to detain him for being drunk, but had somehow lost control of the situation. Now they were struggling to restore their crumbling authority by threatening to bring in the Military Police, to "put him on a charge", even to bring in a loaded weapon – madness to introduce into such chaos.

Bill approached the group, crisply calling the man's name as he came. "Doherty!" Doherty recognised him. "Yessir." "Doherty you're making a fool of yourself there. Put that thing down, and get off to bed." "Yessir." End of fracas. Doherty staggered one way and his would-be detainers the other. A foolish over-indulgence had been prevented from becoming a "federal issue".

There are not many anecdotes about Bill's army experiences, because he seldom talked about the war at all. The fact that this incident was one he recounted means he thought it reflected well upon his self-image. His favourite stories often featured quick-wittedness and a sharp piece of repartee used to good effect. Those were attributes he didn't mind flaunting a little, while he never alluded to more serious qualities – courage, brains, steadfastness – either in relation to others or to himself.

This story shows that Bill, in spite of his youth and inexperience, had acquired the respect of his men. He found the tone to get through to Doherty in his drunk and defiant state. His ease in taking charge from the older and more experienced NCOs, and incidentally giving them a lesson in how to handle authority, is impressive.

CHAPTER 4

Out of the Trenches

Today in the tiny village of Contalmaison in the valley of the river Somme, no sign remains of the devastation of 1915 and 1916 except an immaculately kept war graveyard tucked discreetly out of sight. With neither a shop, a pub to drink in nor anywhere to eat or even post a letter, the little main street is unremittingly tidy, clean and quiet.

There had once been an old manor house, large and impressive, which artillery had smashed to a heap of rubble by 1916. No trace of it can be found today: the young man driving a tractor on the main street had never heard of such a building. On one side of this street, through a brick arch, a courtyard of farm buildings has been converted to holiday gîtes. On the opposite side, where the manor house once stood, is a narrow path leading to a neat cemetery with rows of identical headstones of the war dead, all young men in their teens and twenties with names from Ireland, Scotland, Wales and England and from every part of "the Empire on which the sun never set": India, Canada, South Africa, Australia, New Zealand.

CONTALMAISON MANOR HOUSE BEFORE AND AFTER THE SOMME OFFENSIVE.

There is another imposing reminder of the war in the village. The twin flagpoles beside the church carry the French Tricolour and the diagonal white cross on blue background of the Scottish Saltire. A small plaque beside it explains that this is in memory of the men of the Scots Brigade who fought to their deaths in this tiny village. Our own memorial is the jagged gash in Bill Andrews' helmet, for it was here in Contalmaison that a spinning shard of steel from an exploding shell in the sky split its dome and was diverted only inches from the skull it was intended to shatter. It saved him from his own plot in the manor house graveyard.

On 30th June 1916, the day before the Somme, Contalmaison was much as it is today, the same trim houses and church, but it was deserted as it was in a warzone, just 2 kilometres behind the German lines. The manor house had been an easy target for the artillery, and its grand roof and turrets were destroyed, but its cellar was still used as a refuge for men and materiel. German troops marched on the street and lurked in the deserted houses.

30th June 1916 was Bill Andrews' 24th birthday and he celebrated it with a shouted "cheers" over a cup of tea in the reserve trench. They had

THE CHURCH AT CONTALMAISON.

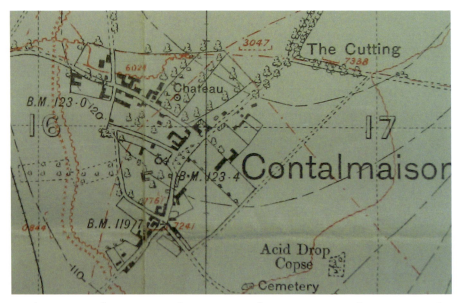

to shout to be heard over the boom of the big guns in the rear and the crash of exploding shells, and their tea rippled with tremors from the vibrating earth. The bombardment had been the most intense ever. It had been running for a week which signalled that they were in for something big.

The British high command's plan for the Somme offensive was to use a massive opening barrage and underground "mines" to eliminate most, if not all, German machine-gun emplacements.

THE DEPRESSION AT FRICOURT CAUSED BY ONE OF THE MASSIVE MINE BOMBS OF 1st JULY 1916.

The pre-war decision of the German high command to put increased emphasis on artillery and their meticulous arrangements for supplying thousands of tons of shells to their rapidly advancing army had given them an advantage which contributed to their sweeping early victories. The allies eventually boosted their artillery to match. That took more than a year, but by 1916 the Somme Offensive was launched with a huge barrage which heralded allied artillery superiority.

The actual moment of the explosion of a German shrapnel shell in flight is caught in this photograph, raining shards of metal down on the infantry.

THE BATTLEFIELD, A SHRAPNEL SHELL EXPLODING IN MID-AIR.

By the time World War I started, a devilish array of ingenious weaponry was ranged against the helmeted foot soldier. The British army had perfected rapid rifle fire from ranks of well-drilled infantry in preference to the machine gun, which they rejected until 1914 as too heavy and static for the type of offensive war of movement that they favoured. The Germans recognised the machine gun's potential and created specialist machine-gun companies to support their infantry. The weapon had existed for some years, but not until World War I was its ability to transform warfare first exploited. The machine gun's principle was simply to employ the recoil gas from one round to operate a mechanism to load the next round into the breech. Thus they did not need any cranking or external power to operate. The bullets were fed in on long belts. The rate of fire could be as high as 600 rounds per minute, although in practice the rate was nearer to half that. They needed cooling with water or air to prevent overheating – a gunner learned the technique of firing short bursts to reduce the rate of temperature

GERMAN MACHINE-GUN CREW

rise. At 60 to 70kg they were cumbersome to manhandle and needed a wheeled support to move from place to place. Water-cooled machine guns required water supplies to be brought forward in addition to the weighty and rapidly consumed ammunition belts. As the war progressed, lighter, air-cooled machine guns were developed, even handheld versions as light as 9 kg.

The British high command failed to appreciate that by 1916 the Germans had held roughly the same line for more than a year and in that time their strategy had changed from seeking a quick offensive victory in France to conducting a holding campaign to defend the gains they had already made. For this defensive role they had hardened their front line where it stood, with well-built dugouts and deep concrete bunkers, intending to hold the line until they had finished dealing with the Russians on their eastern front.

The 7-day Allied barrage that started the Somme offensive did not penetrate the deep German bunkers even if it did shatter trenches and barbed-wire alike, and it was in those deep shelters that German machine-gunners remained throughout the barrage. They had enough time at the end of it to climb out and get back to their guns in the ten-minute interval between the lifting of the barrage and the start of the infantry assault. Most machine guns were manned and functioning in time to rake the attackers struggling across no-man's-land.

That interval, post-barrage, was a deliberate decision of the British high command: it was a seriously flawed decision and a major cause of the dreadful losses.

The men knew that the coming battle would be a tough one, but had no inkling that they were about to set a world record for casualties that would last to the present day. When they heard that the start time was 7.30 in the morning, in full daylight, a quiver of fear hit them: there was no way out now. The first of July dawned, the bombardment suddenly ceased at 7.20, just hours after the birthday party. The short-lived silence was broken by fourteen massive underground explosions, "mines" under the German trenches, which could be heard as far away as London, signalling the start of the advance and alerting the German soldiers, still hiding in their underground bunkers, to rush to re-man their machine guns. They were in time to mow down the slow-moving masses of British troops caught in the open among the mud-filled shellholes and tangled barbed wire made impassable by their own bombardment. On that day the Allied army suffered more deaths and injuries than has been inflicted in one day's battle ever before or since, nearly 60,000 men in all, 25,000 of them killed.

BRITISH TROOPS PREPARED FOR FURTHER COMBAT.

It was not entirely in vain. The Germans were caught in their trenches at the centre of the front, between Fricourt and Maricourt, and were driven back with bayonets and bullets. Mametz Wood in the middle of this front was a German stronghold and was fought over foot by foot over the next ten days. Five thousand Welsh Fusiliers lost their lives clearing the Germans from the wood which was within machine-gun range of Contalmaison. The battle ranged over the ground around Contalmaison for several days before the final push into the village on 10th July.

The "Sappers" was the British Army's corps for construction; Bill's function was to do the army's building work. On 10th July 1916, his section of the 128th Field Company took up position in trenches immediately behind the infantry who were to launch an assault at 3.30 pm to take Contalmaison village.

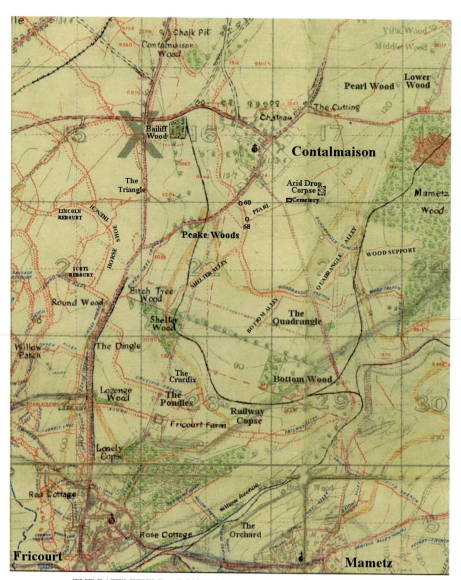

THE BATTLEFIELD AROUND CONTALMAISON, 10th JULY 1916.

Out of the Trenches

The order setting out Bill's unit's role was issued the day before; that order is shown here.

23 rd Division – C.R.S. Order No. S.8.   9. 7.16.

(1) The 69th Infantry Brigade is to attack CONTALMAISON from the west tomorrow evening.

(2) One section of 128th Field Coy. R.E. will report to 9th YORKS Regt. at 3.30.p.m. on 10.7.16 at X.15.c.9.9. to assist in consolidation of a post at X.16.b.4.3. Route via SAUSAGE Valley to X.20.b.4.5. and then up communication trench to above assembly point.

(3) The 101st Field Coy. less H.Q. and 128th Field Coy. less one section and H.Q. will assemble in trench at X.21.c.5.8 at 4.p.m. on 10.7.16. The 128th Field Coy. Will leave one officer in billets to command the H.Q. of both Coys.

(4) On G.O.C. 69th Brigade informing when the Coys. are to move up, orders will be sent to them via 69th Bde. Advanced H.Qrs. at Scots Redoubt X.21.c.9.9. The 128th Field Coy. will consolidate the Manor House buildings at X.17.c.2.8. and the 101st Field Coy. will consolidate in the vicinity of Cross Roads at X.16.d.8.4. The Coys. less one section 128th Field Coy. will report to G.O.C. 69th Bde. at Scots Redoubt for orders as to route to be followed into CONTALMAISON.

(5) The R.E. working parties in (2) and (3) will be withdrawn before dawn.

(6) Instructions re material will be issued later.

(7) One day's rations in addition to the Iron ration will be carried.
Overcoats will not be carried.

(8) Reports to C.R.E. at Divisional H.Q. via H.Q. 69th Infantry Bde.

                                      O.G.Brennin.
                                      Lieut: Colonel R.E.
                                      C.R.E. 23 rd Division.

Issued at 7.00 a.m. 10/7/16 by messenger

                BILL'S COMPANY'S ORDERS FOR 10th JULY 1916

Some of the instructions on this order seem extraordinary at first sight, the need to be poised to move forward immediately after an assault by infantry to capture the small village, the necessity to withdraw before dawn the next day.

One of the principal functions of Sapper Field Companies was to construct machine gun emplacements in newly taken territory. It was an

AWAITING THE ORDER.

urgent task because of the possibility of early counter-attacks. Infantry in newly taken territory had no trenches to shelter in and no barbed wire in front to obstruct a counter-attack and they had no cover from machine guns until these were brought forward. The machine guns were heavy and needed fortified emplacements from which to fire. It was possible for a well-organised enemy to take advantage of this by launching a quick counter-attack.

Reserves were held by all armies for exactly that purpose. From the moment that new territory was captured, a deadly game of redeployment and counter-attack began, orchestrated by the generals in their headquarters behind the lines. The speed with which a counter-attack could be launched depended on how close the reserves were to the location of the enemy breakthrough; the advancing army had to quickly secure the gained ground with barbed wire and strongpoints to repulse the counter-play. This was Bill's unit's job. The work of setting up machine-gun emplacements and barbed-wire defences was referred to as "consolidation". Machine-gun emplacements were always a prime target for artillery, so the emplacements were located where they would be as inconspicuous as possible. Construction work on them took place under cover of darkness so that enemy observers would not see it. This explains why the order specifies withdrawal of the Sappers "before dawn".

The Sappers did not take part in the actual assault which captured the village – this was the job of the infantry, the 8th and 9th Green Howards supported by the 11th West Yorks – but waited in the trench for word that the village was taken before moving forward. At this time they tightened their Brodie helmets on their heads and Bill gave himself the added protection of muttering the St Patrick's Breastplate under his breath. They were equipped for building, not fighting – and their orders were to work for the whole of the coming night, to create a machine-gun strongpoint in front of the captured village in the ruins of the old manor house and to put up barbed-wire entanglements in the new no-man's-land.

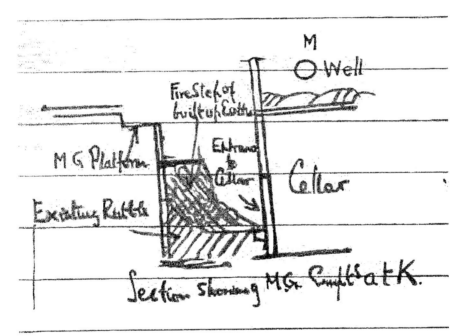

ARMY FIELD SKETCH OF THE MACHINE-GUN EMPLACEMENT THAT BILL AND HIS
MEN WERE CONSTRUCTING ON THE NIGHT OF 10th JULY 1916.

CONTALMAISON CAPTURED BY NIGHT ATTACK; HUNS FAIL TO REGAIN VILLAGE

British Take Several Hundred Prisoners and are Pushing Ahead in Other Directions Now—Infantry Too Close for Guns to Fire at First Line—Description of Fight

Special Star Cable.

LONDON, July 11.—The news of the capture of Contalmaison, which was made public through Gen. Haig's report to the War Office today, sent a thrill of quiet satisfaction through the public, which has been watching the development of fighting around this keenly-disputed position with the most intense interest for the past few days. The capture of several hundred prisoners is also a feature of the report that has given cause for congratulation.

The official statement says:—

"Last night, after a brisk bombardment, our infantry attack carried Contalmaison by assault, taking 189 unwounded prisoners, including a battalion commander and four other officers.

"A strong counter-attack, delivered by the Germans during the night, was beaten back with heavy loss to the enemy, and the whole village is now in our hands.

"Further east we stormed several lines of trenches in the Bois de Mametz, and the greater part of this large wood is now in our possession. Here we captured one heavy howitzer, three field guns and 296 unwounded prisoners, including three officers.

"Heavy fighting continues in Trones wood. In continuation of the report on aerial combats on July 9, one of our aeroplanes was shot down by a direct hit from an anti-aircraft gun, and three other machines have not returned to our lines."

The French War Office announced this afternoon that the night had passed without important fighting on the French front on each side of the Somme. In the fighting of the last two days the French took 1,000 prisoners.

Bill's own helmet had only been issued to him 2 weeks previously, just before the Somme Offensive. It was of the second phase of Brodie's design, with toughened steel and matt paint to reduce its visibility. A thickening of the edge of the brim was added later because the original edge was so thin that it caused cuts and eye damage when men stumbled upon each other in the dark trenches. Bill's helmet was missing this modification: its brim had the early sharp edge. It was produced in the factory of Thomas Firth and Sons in Sheffield in 1915.

The metal of the helmet does not rest directly on the wearer's head. The layering between head and metal is sophisticated, with a padded cap resting directly on the head and a series of canvas straps which hold the steel shell just out of contact with the padding. The effect of all this is that when the steel bowl is struck with enough force to distort the metal, the whole shell takes up the impact and distributes it over a large area of padding so that the impact on the skull is spread and greatly dissipated. This is what saved Bill's life.

Complaints from the soldiers about the Brodie helmet concerned the "inside work", the padding and straps which, in the earlier helmets, were of poor quality and uncomfortable to wear and were altered in later versions with additional linen layers. This difficulty, rather than a dandified taste for individuality, explains the fashion among some officers to have their London tailors carry out alterations to the linings of their helmets when home on leave. A Pall Mall tailor would provide a silk lining tailored to the individual's cranium. Bill's helmet had no such tinkering, it was the standard issue given to the army's millions.

There is a theory among various factions in Bill's family that the helmet was a superfluous adornment in Bill's case, as he and all his male descendants are equipped with some of the most resilient skulls in Europe. Motor cycle accidents, low-clearance staircases, wallops on marble mantle shelves and steel girders alike have demonstrated this resilience. It is not a theory with which the authors concur.

At 3.30 the Green Howards made the direct attack on the village in a wide sweep of 1,000 yards from the west. At the same time the West Yorks delivered a flanking assault from the left. Between them they caught the German troops in a pincer attack and forced them to retreat under heavy fire. At 4.30 the Green Howards gained a foothold in Contalmaison village, and by 5.30 the West Yorks had joined them. They suffered disastrous casualties in this attack, as severe as any in the Somme offensive, and in those two hours the 8th Green Howards lost nearly half their men and two-thirds of their officers.

THE MOMENT OF TRUTH.

All this time, Bill's section was parked in their trench, ready for action, hearing the shots and din of the charge at the enemy, the rattle of machine-gun fire, the thump and boom of incoming shells. They listened out for the sounds of a reversal but none came and they felt both relief and fear, safe for the moment but doomed to a night in the open. They kept totally silent themselves, on orders not to make a target, although the din of battle was everywhere.

Out of the Trenches

At 5.30 the word came through – the attack had gained ground and they had to secure it. They were shifted forward to the front-line trench and saw ruined buildings above as they pushed closer to the din of battle. But still they had to wait, this time for darkness to fall. At 9.00 the light in the sky was dimming when the Germans counter-attacked. The shelling increased, they heard rifle fire and machine-guns and the boom of hand-thrown grenades. The front-line infantry were well supplied with these "bombs" and they threw them forward and fired at the shadows in the evening gloom. The German counter-attack continued in starts and spurts for half-an-hour and then died away.

Then the order the Sappers had been dreading came up the line, "Move Forward". This was the real test of courage. The little security they had felt in the trench had to be thrown to the wind and their bodies exposed completely in the open. Bill showed outward calm as he stepped over the parapet. One by one the men followed, their pace slowed by the weight of their loads. They were now completely exposed in ground that until a few moments ago had been too dangerous even to look at because of the chance of a bullet. They trudged forward, burdened with picks and shovels and rolls of barbed wire.

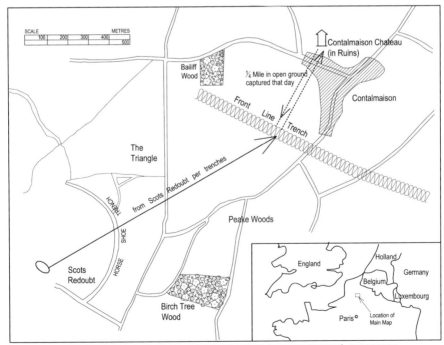

THE ROUTE TO CONTALMAISON MANOR HOUSE ON 10th JULY 1916.

CONTALMAISON VILLAGE AFTER THE BATTLE.

The artillery did not spot its target and take aim. Its target was just a compass line and distance. They didn't select their own targets and quite usually didn't even see them. This shelling never stopped, day or night, up and down the lines. The din of cannon fire and explosions was the constant backdrop to the battle but at any one point on the front line its intensity ebbed and flowed and the troops were highly attuned to the sound of the missiles that mattered to them, the whine of close-by shells or the approach of a creeping bombardment. They were especially alert for the dull thud, sounding like a failed explosion, of a gas shell.

A high proportion of casualties on the Allied side were head injuries from shrapnel shells. The explosive charge is in the base, the shrapnel above it, a mass of metal spheres of steel or lead the size of large marbles. Shrapnel shells were timed to explode in flight, raining these balls at deadly speed on exposed men, spreading out like shotgun pellets.

Any inaccuracy in the firing settings was made up for by the vast numbers of shells fired. Bill had seen the vast stocks of shells and the bulldozed mountains of spent shell casings and he knew that the Germans had equal or greater supplies in their armoury.

The timer was in the front of the shells for ease of access when firing and had to be set to explode when the shell was over an enemy position. It ignited a tube of explosive down the middle of the shell which in turn detonated the main charge at the rear, throwing out the deadly balls of metal. The fuse was normally completely destroyed in the shell-burst, but if it misfired and remained intact it was a valuable source of information. If a soldier found a timer-fuse from an enemy shell he was expected to get it straight back to his own artillerymen who could use its setting to locate and target the battery that had fired it. Shrapnel had caused more casualties by the end of the war than small arms fire, even including the deadly machine guns. In this sense the damage to Bill's helmet was a characteristically World War I hit.

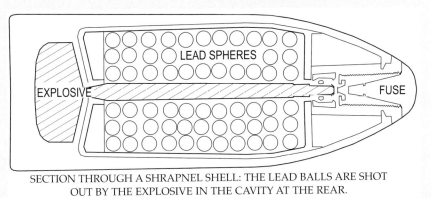

SECTION THROUGH A SHRAPNEL SHELL: THE LEAD BALLS ARE SHOT OUT BY THE EXPLOSIVE IN THE CAVITY AT THE REAR.

Shells exploded around them and overhead, raining down spinning shards of shrapnel, jagged bits of shell casings mixed with lead balls designed to kill, their mass and velocity carefully calculated for lethal impact. It was bad enough to be exposed to the random aim of this weaponry, but now the men were right at the heart of the day's action, the nighttime target to buy time for the dawn counterattack.

The first gut-searing terror gradually softened as the Sappers realised that death was not inevitable. They glanced around and saw their comrades unharmed and looking out for one another. The July night was short and overcast and maybe they would make it through. It was now black dark and the damp and mist of the night rose from the shellholes and the mud. They found their objective, the ruins of Contalmaison manor house, and set about their work, moving earth and stones, building caves in the cellar to protect the machine-gunners and still give them a good range of fire. Bill's job as the Lieutenant-Engineer was to keep control on the construction work so that the machine-gun emplacement bore some resemblance to the drawing provided in his orders. It was not quite the same as digging a manhole in central London or building a pump-house in Edinburgh, but the objective was the same. Measurement was by arms' lengths, by touch in the blind black night, the measuring arm always in danger of being pinioned by a pick. Small details were important, a narrow opening for the gun but with a wide degree of movement for the barrel, enough room for the two-man gun team, one firing, the other feeding in the belts, with a space on the other side for spent cartridges.

Maintaining building standards in the dark and under fire was not what he had learnt at university, but it was what Bill was good at: improvisation and coping and making the best of what he had. Some of the men had better eyesight in the dark than others, poachers or nightwatchmen in another world, and he had to make best use of their talents.

The bond of teamwork and comradeship could overreach itself, making some of the men cocky and keen and heedless of risk, showing their bravado. Instead of flattening themselves at the sound of a shell, they'd keep the picks swinging and the earth flying. This had to be controlled – keep them working *and* safe – and Bill's judgement was tested to the limit.

THE REMAINS OF A GERMAN MACHINE-GUN EMPLACEMENT, PHOTO NOV 2012.

Out of the Trenches

Many years later, at a reunion of what was left of his Field Company, Bill made it the one occasion when he brought his wife Christina to such an event: he was concerned with the dwindling numbers of his comrades and wanted her to meet them while they were still cogent. She was asked the next day by her son what it was like and her eyes welled with tears. "They had such respect for Bill," she said with surprise and esteem in her voice. One old soldier, a sergeant in the regular army before the war, had enumerated all the reasons why this young graduate should have been totally unsuited to leading his men in the field of battle: he was young, Irish, a recent graduate from university, a qualified engineer with little site experience and none in combat, and yet he stood up and calmly led them out of the trench and they, old hands and raw recruits alike, simply followed his lead.

It took respect like this to enable Bill to do his job and the respect grew with the work. No doubt there were casualties that night, those past hope to be left where they fell, the injured taking two good men out of the working party to ferry them back to safety. Time passed quickly and dawn was approaching when they shouldered their shovels and sledges, picks and pincers and marched for home. Still in silence they crossed the newly captured stretch that had been yesterday's no-man's-land.

Another shell exploded close behind them and they pitched themselves forward in the mud, metal shards flailing around their ears. As they clambered to their feet, one of them stopped and waved furiously at the mud.

"The lieutenant's hit," he shouted. Bill was flat out on his face. They felt his back and his face and found the gash in the back of the helmet. "He's breathing." The urge to leave him there was strong but comradeship and duty won out and two of them lifted his arms and hoisted him between them. They dragged him along, his limp body weighing heavily, the helmet pulling his head down and whacking against their arms and bodies. They got to the trench where helping hands lowered him down. He lay in the bottom of the trench while the stretcher-bearers were called up and somebody eased the helmet off his head. The stretcher-bearers arrived and strapped Bill onto the stretcher. One of them made to throw away the helmet as Bill was slowly coming round. He saw what was happening. "Give it here to me," he said, "It saved my life. I'm going to preserve it."

The men obeyed. With the helmet on his chest rather than his head, Bill was carried away.

According to ballistics experts who examined the damage, the missile that hit Bill's helmet was sharp; its impact left a characteristic indent. That rules out lead or steel balls of purpose-made shrapnel; the experts suggested a jagged fragment of a shell's casing. It is the back of the helmet that the shrapnel hit; the point of impact is the junction of brim and crown. Its sharpness caught the brim and tore open the gash; a rounded missile might have glanced off and caused distortion only; Brodie's generous brim ensured that it didn't plunge straight into the back of Bill's neck. The helmet's damage gives no hint as to the type of German gun that fired the shell.

Out of the Trenches

Bill's own accounts of this near-death experience, a sharp missile halted within fractions of an inch of his skull, were always told with a touch of irony, the stretcher-bearers reluctantly accepting the added burden of a useless tin hat on the say-so of the dazed lieutenant. He was pleased that he'd had the wit and decisiveness to overcome the stretcher-bearers' reluctance to add a spent helmet to their load and the presence of mind that saved the helmet from becoming another item of battle debris. He kept that helmet safe for the rest of his life. He never described how he felt when the full import of his scrape with death hit him, whether he lapsed into shock or grief or ecstasy at his narrow escape or just shrugged it off as battlefield luck, but he understood well his unbelievable good fortune to be the one among thousands to have felt a direct hit at the Somme and survived to tell the tale.

The Company War Diary shows that he was back in the trenches after eighteen days: the bald one-line entry for the 28th July in the war diary of the 128th Field Company reads:

"LT. W. P. ANDREWS REJOINED FOR DUTY WITH THE COY."
WAR DIARY ENTRY, 128th FIELD COY, FOR 28th JULY 1916.

CHAPTER 5

Mespot

This book probably gives more importance to the day the helmet was split open than Bill did himself. To him it was an event on the battlefield which he survived and put behind him. He served in the army from 1915 until his demobilisation in the spring of 1919, and after getting his good tin hat ruined on 10th July 1916, his experiences included widely varying episodes: winning the Military Cross, an award for gallantry; having it pinned on his chest by the King Emperor, George V, in Buckingham Palace; being rushed from the front to London for treatment for a life-threatening lung disease contracted in the trenches; strange practices in a military warehouse; being posted to Iraq – which he always referred to as Mespot – and fighting a very gentlemanly war against the Turks there; being accused of mutiny, and more.

BILL'S MILITARY CROSS.

His Military Cross seems to have been awarded for carrying out his duties with consistent bravery and "doing his duty" in or out of danger at the front line, rather than for any one spectacular feat of der-ring-do. His job was construction, which does not sound either dangerous or demanding of outstanding bravery, but as the incident of the shrapnel and the helmet in the last chapter illustrates, he and his section routinely undertook work in front of their own front line. Whenever new territory was taken, the first troops sent into it were the Sappers. Newly gained territory had to be "consolidated" before a German counter-attack could recover it and the Sappers worked in front of the existing front line, to create a new, advanced one. They were both exposed to any enemy sniper fire within range and unprotected from the constant shellfire. Their work could only be

GEORGE V PRESENTING AWARDS AT THE FRONT IN FRANCE.

attempted at night without showing any light; the dark prevented accurate sniper fire, but artillery fired "blind" and the gunners didn't see their targets as they fired – they were given a direction (compass bearing) and a range (distance) – and this meant their fire was as accurate at night as during the day. Every time an advance was achieved, Bill's section had to venture into the open for as long as it took to carry out their tasks. On 10th July, for instance, this exposure lasted from sunset to sunrise next morning, seven or eight hours, whereas the average survival time in the open was a matter of hours or minutes.

The most important quality an officer could have in these circumstances was durability. He had to complete dangerous tasks as ordered, not just on one great occasion, but again and again unflinchingly. He had to remain undeterred by the mounting casualty list and the growing aggregate of his own time spent "in the open." It was because Bill could be counted upon to keep on leading his men calmly out of the trenches for sortie after sortie, even after having the helmet on his head cracked open by shrapnel, that he became marked out as "the man who deserves a medal if anyone does."

He made fun of being awarded it, saying he got it because he was able to get beer for the colonel when no one else could. He seemed to feel that so many had died, in many instances died with bravery after enduring years of danger, that the survivors should not look for a lifetime's recognition for doing just the same tasks but having had the luck not to fall. At the same time he did value his Military Cross. The hardship and danger he had sustained, and the way he had handled his command, had fully earned the award. As it happened he was very near to joining the fatal casualties before George V got to pin the Military Cross on his tunic.

He was once persuaded by his three inquisitive sons, twenty or more years after the events, to explain the army's process of selection for awards. One officer in each unit was assigned the job. Naturally this was a fairly senior officer – the matter was taken seriously; but that created a difficulty in that senior officers were not often at the front line during actions. Did a lot of people want to get medals? we asked. Oh Yes. Bill

BUCKINGHAM PALACE.

chuckled at the memory. Some men became obsessed with them. He'd seen men do crazy things when the awarding officer was at the front, hoping to catch his eye. Bill regarded that as madness. It was easy even for his children to see that if courageous actions were taking place ahead of the front line, and in the dark as well, the awarding officer had quite a problem in trying to see every single act of bravery.

It may have been when his sons were talking to him at that time that one of us asked, "How could anyone go out into no-man's-land to work without being killed immediately?" As I recall his response I feel a shiver go down my spine. There was silence. The fifty-year-old was recalling events of long ago. For a few seconds he was unaware of his sons around him, while memories of terrible events flooded in on him. He said nothing. He left us no wiser. The memories overwhelmed him. Little wonder that it was so seldom he could bring himself to talk about the war. A second, piped-up question produced the same effect: "Did you ever shoot anyone in the war?" No, he didn't kill anyone, he replied gravely. "Thank God," he added and once again he didn't advance any enlightenment.

THE LONDON CROWD 1917. AMERICA HAS JUST JOINED THE WAR.

His next recorded brush with death after the helmet saved his life at Contalmaison was not from enemy action but from the conditions at the front. Again, we don't know the time or the place where he contracted pleurisy, "a disease causing inflammation of the lining of the lungs," but the disease did very nearly kill him. He was hustled back to one of the famous hospitals in London. He recovered to the extent that he was able to leave hospital and live a normal life, but the function of one half of one of his lungs had been lost irretrievably. As a result, his Medical Category was revised down to "unfit for field service" – that is, for battle. The immediate effect of this was to get him out of the trenches in France and he seemed to have been mildly relieved rather than ecstatic about that. More gravely, the disease lurked within him for the rest of his life, slowly affecting his remaining lung capacity and robbing him of his breath until it finally claimed his life when he was 68. There is no doubt that, without it, he would have enjoyed a longer active life. No one can recall his ever complaining about it. If he had not had it he would probably have continued to serve at the front where every day held the risk of death. Also, once he was demobilised three years later, he received a partial disability allowance which lasted for the rest of his life and his widow received a pension related to it after his death 40 years later. The pleurisy also ensured that he would be in England and close enough to London to attend Buckingham Palace for the award of his Military Cross by the king. Not by any means every award was presented by His Majesty; there were far too many. The vast majority were presented by the recipient's commanding officer. We would like to think that a handshake with the King Emperor may have been reserved for the more highly regarded.

After his recovery from pleurisy and medical downgrade he was given the sort of soft, easy assignment that every reluctant recruit dreamed of; and Bill hated. He once described the working day: each day, without exception, the cohort of officers stationed at The Depot, somewhere near London, would pass the time, totally unoccupied, for 6 hours. They were given no instructions, duties or responsibilities. At 4 o'clock in the

TROOPS RELAXING, PLAYING FOOTBALL, 1917.

afternoon, each day, they were brought together in an office and set at desks. An orderly then brought in a huge pile of dockets. Each docket had to receive an officer's signature and this process had to be completed against a tight deadline. Every officer received an unsorted portion of the big bundle and this had to be completed against the deadline. Signature was the *only* requirement. The dockets were not read, much less checked. They were signed. It was necessary to work quickly to get through the quota. For twenty minutes or so they scribbled their names on dockets which were then immediately reassembled and whisked away. That finished their duties for the day. Every working day. It was not long before the young officer who had shown his mettle at the front on The Somme – and won a Military Cross – found the waste of his time and talents, not to mention the boredom, intolerable.

His suggestions to give the work more meaning – or more use, for instance that they should get the dockets earlier so that, at least, they could know what they signified and what their purpose was – any such idea was rejected as if he were proposing sabotage. Bill suggested that some of the officers might help to deal with matters on the warehouse dispatch floor. The idea was rejected with horror; any such "interference" with the work was strictly forbidden. "They'd be on strike within hours." The routine was to be adhered to. It was set in stone.

NORMAL LIFE CONTINUED BACK HOME: LUNCHTIME 1917.

BILL'S MEDAL CARD: THIS SHOWS THAT WHEN HE WAS AWARDED THE MILITARY CROSS HE HAD BEEN PROMOTED TO ACTING CAPTAIN.

It seems that regulations stated that every consignment dispatched should be checked by an independent officer who would ensure that the consignment did in fact contain everything listed on the accompanying docket, and then sign the docket.

Those who were running the depot apparently had good reason NOT to have the dockets checked. (Apparently they were also carrying on a long tradition. Pepys, the "father" of the Royal Navy, was induced to take his original post at the Admiralty during Charles II's reign in the seventeenth century because he was assured of profitable patronage over suppliers. He rooked them mercilessly too.) His twentieth-century counterparts had much stronger motivation than those who tried to prevent their shenanigans. It appears that the whole management of the depot was in the hands of those who were making a dishonest dollar by means of well-organised corruption. They had devised and set up the "signing factory" Bill now found himself part of, which ensured that every delivery was accompanied by a docket which was indeed signed by an officer, and yet the deliveries went out absolutely unchecked. Such a set-up would explain the alarm caused by any move on the part of the signing officers that they should actually do the job they were meant to.

Uncle Bill's Tin Hat

Bill did not match the management's concept of the perfect officer. Independent-minded and with a forceful personality, he was the opposite of the battle-shy puppets they preferred. Bill, for his part, started trying to get away from this stultifying existence – even to the extent of requesting a return to his old unit in the trenches. Perhaps the Depot's management had enough influence to have him posted as far away from their depot as was militarily feasible.

This may explain the next event in Bill's army career. Otherwise it seems totally inexplicable. The "medically unfit for field service" officer was posted to a force being dispatched to fight the Turks in Mesopotamia! Perhaps the Depot's management was able to have his medical category "not noticed" when such things were being checked for his posting to Mespot.

But first, Lieutenant Andrews, having been awarded the Military Cross for valour at the front in France, and since he was in England anyway, was instructed to attend for presentation of said Gong by one Sailor George V, who was the King Emperor, at Buckingham Palace on 25th April 1917. The date is embossed on the back of the Cross, so, for once, we do know its exact date.

When Bill spoke of that occasion, it was of its ludicrous aspect that he most relished telling. The build-up was impressive, uniforms were made spotless, every detail of dress was specified and inspected scrupulously in advance. The ceremonial itself was simple: a hooking on of the medal, quick handshake and murmur of congratulations. Following it, the recipients, feeling honoured and distinguished, floated out of the Presence Chamber to an ante-room. As Bill stepped through the door, someone snatched the cross from his tunic. For a second Bill thought he was being mugged in the precincts of the palace. A flunky (Bill's term for him) was standing just inside the door and had snatched the Cross unceremoniously and without a word. As Bill turned to him in surprise the flunky turned his back. Another, beside him, held out a medal box, the Cross was slapped into it, the lid snapped shut and the box returned peremptorily to the hero who, thirty seconds earlier, was being honoured by his Emperor. Bill said it was the promptest cutting-down to size that the authorities could possibly have achieved.

He returned from this sumptuous and heart-warming celebration of his valour to the Depot where he signed dockets. Mespot awaited him.

Sadly, Bill's mother, Mary Ellen, had died only six weeks before his visit to Buckingham Palace. She died in the Governor's House in Cork City Gaol with her husband, William senior, at her side. She had been told of the Military Cross her youngest son had won for bravery, and of his forthcoming encounter with the king, but the cancer (of the liver) brought her busy and energetic life to an end too soon.

The question of reconciling Irish patriotism with British Army service arose for Bill at times. One of these occasions was when news of the 1916 rising in Dublin reached the front. Bill once recounted what happened in the mess in France. He recalled that in the officers' mess the comment was

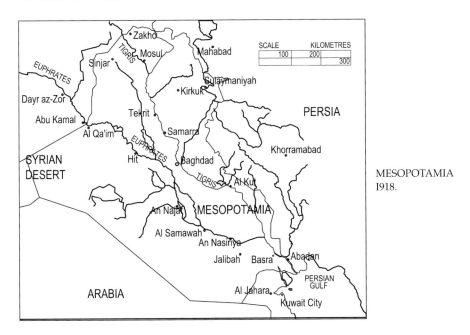

MESOPOTAMIA 1918.

predictable. The rebels in Dublin were condemned for unforgivable treachery. No trace of mitigation, much less justification, was conceivable to the officers who were enduring a terrifying and horrible war. Bill's inclination was to stay clear of any discussion, but eventually he was drawn to intervene. He attempted to explain the rebels' cause or at least that they were acting out of the same patriotism to their own country that the World War I participants had for theirs. The upshot was that he was called outside by his commanding officer, who remonstrated with him. "What you are saying could very well constitute mutiny, Andrews. You should be very careful,…" That is all Bill said about the occasion. It is clear that in the chest of the young Royal Engineer lieutenant there beat an Irish heart. His actions at the end of the war give more evidence of it.

So, wounded and unfit for active service, the next step in his army career was to sail to Mespot to fight the Turks.

In early 1917 Bill was still in England – the date on the back of the Military Cross places him here. At some subsequent date that year he sailed in a convoy carrying an expeditionary force from Liverpool to Basra to take part in the war in Mespot.

"Mespot" was the army abbreviation for Mesopotamia, the land between the rivers. It was an Ottoman Empire possession. That Empire, with its capital in Istanbul, had been drawn into the war on the German side against Britain in 1916. Basra is the only seaport in Mespot. (Bill always pronounced it, as if parodying Army usage, with an explosive 'Rah!'). All

THE TROOPS IN MESPOT: NOTE SOME ARE WEARING PITH HELMETS INSTEAD OF THE STANDARD BRODIE HELMET.

the British forces for Mespot arrived through it. It lies at the extreme inner end of the Persian Gulf, and in the southernmost part of Mespot. It is 80 kilometres inland from the Gulf, accessed from the coast via the Shatt-al-Arab channel. The war in Mespot had started in this vicinity with a landing in 1914 of British Forces from India*.

The voyage from Liverpool to Basra, the port for Mespot, was long and slow. They travelled in convoy, uneventfully in the military sense, from Liverpool around the Cape of Good Hope, passing Cape Town to port,

---

* Although fighting started in 1914, neither side "declared war" on the other until 1916. The Turks had for a while considered entering the war on the Allied side.

Mespot

CASUALTIES ON THE MESOPOTAMIAN CAMPAIGN.

north across the Indian Ocean, into the Persian Gulf and through the Gulf's entire length, to Basra. The shorter route through the Mediterranean and the Suez Canal was deemed too dangerous; Axis navies lurked there, both German and Austrian. For Bill the voyage was fixed in his recollections by the two new attributes he acquired on the oceans – the ability to play a good and highly aggressive hand of Bridge and a taste for whiskey. These were attributes which remained with him for the rest of his days.

By late 1917, when Bill arrived, the British had advanced – having taken a number of substantial knocks along the way – a very long way up the River Tigris. In the spring of 1917 they had taken Baghdad, 500km from Basra, and were now fighting their way still further north. Their final goal was to be Mosul, where oil had been found, a further 320km upriver. So, when Bill's expeditionary force disembarked at Basra in 1917, after a very long voyage, they still had a long, long inland journey ahead of them to reach the front line. Roads were virtually non-existent in Mespot; the two rivers were the main transport routes.

Bill recalled his introduction to the military situation when he finally reached the front. He and his guide, another officer, set off on horseback. As they rode out, the guide pointed out various British "forward" emplacements and the ride continued. Bill, whose only previous experience of war had been in France where the front lines could be as little as fifty yards apart and snipers terrorised everyone for some distance behind the front line, began to feel uncomfortable. "Aren't we too far forward to be on horseback? Nearing the front line?" "Oh we passed our front line half a mile back. Turks' is somewhere over there." This was a very different form of warfare, but it was deadly nonetheless.

This campaign is little written about. As combat experience, Bill found it infinitely less tense, dangerous or life-threatening than the trenches in France. The climate, at least in the dry season, was a great deal more pleasant than that of northern France. As a result of how he talked about it, the impression we obtained was that this was not a hard-fought campaign, but that was very far from being the case.

The British Army was involved in Mesopotamia from the very beginning of the war. There were two reasons for the intervention. Firstly, there was an oil refinery belonging to the Anglo-Persian Oil Company at Abadan, on the Shatt-al-Arab (it was one of the world's earliest oil refineries). The Royal Navy needed its output. Secondly, the India office of the British Empire in Delhi was now eyeing Mespot, having successfully acquired effective control of both Persia (modern-day Iran) and Egypt.

The initial invasion of Mespot was undertaken from Delhi with units from the British Army and the Indian Army. The original invasion force sailed from India on 16th October 1914. It established a bridgehead, and on 21st November 1914 Basra was captured. At this time there was only a small peace-time Turkish garrison in Basra; the Turks had not expected this invasion. Their small garrison force retreated inland along the river Tigris. The British/Indians began to follow this retreat and the Turks eventually reinforced the units opposing them. There followed a campaign, or rather a series of campaigns, separated by considerable intervals, which lasted for

A WARSHIP IN THE SHATT-AL-ARAB.

the full duration of the war. Although it was fought in a very different fashion from the war in France, there was very tough Turkish resistance, and, in 1916, the British suffered severe losses including, on 29th April that year, the humiliation of the surrender of a force of 13,164 men which habeen cut off at Kut-al-Amara, 150km upstream from Basra on the Tigris. Desperate attempts to break out from Kut and several relief sorties from Basra had all been repulsed by the besieging Turks. Following this, there was for a time a serious threat that the Turks would drive the British back into the sea. This was averted and there was a major reorganisation of the British forces and

THE HORSE WAS IN ITS ELEMENT IN THE WAR IN MESPOT.

their infrastructure. A second, successful advance commenced on 13th December 1916, along the Tigris. It retook Kut-al-Amara (the captured troops had long since been marched away – apparently few of them survived captivity) and continued on to Baghdad. The Indian Army played a significant role in the taking of Baghdad on 13th March 1917, after which the advance checked. All told, casualties for the British/Indians in the Mesopotamian campaign came to 92,000; Turkish casualties are unknown, but 45,000 Turkish prisoners of war were known to have been taken. The casualty figures at least are an indication of how deadly and bitter a campaign it had been.

There is a photograph of Bill in Mespot, probably newly arrived, taken in 1917 with a number of other British officers, all captains. That rank indicates that they had been in the army for some time – they weren't fresh from cadet school. Two things stand out. Looking at the faces, Bill's shows the marks of his combat service in the trenches. He has a tougher, perhaps warier, expression than any of the others. This impression is borne out by the decorations on his uniform and the lack of them on the

BILL, SECOND FROM LEFT, FRONT ROW, WITH FELLOW NEW ARRIVALS TO THE MESOPOTAMIA. NOTE HOW HE HAS AGED IN THE TWO YEARS SINCE THE PHOTO ON PAGE 34.

BILL, TOP RIGHT, AND FELLOW OFFICERS IN MESPOT.

others'. Bill is the only one of them with any medal or decoration. His Military Cross stands out and it is accompanied by another ribbon declaring him to be a 1915 volunteer rather than a conscript.

It is quite clear that it was well after the taking of Baghdad in March 1917 that he arrived, because he was still collecting his award in London six weeks after that date. The Turks, when they'd been ousted from Baghdad, had moved their army headquarters to Mosul, even further upriver. Bill recounted how on one occasion he had a vantage point on high ground from which he was able to watch a whole British army advancing; while he watched, it split into two columns which diverged and encircled the enemy force in a classic pincer movement.

TRANSPORT WAS MAINLY BY RIVER IN THE MESOPOTAMIAN CAMPAIGN.

The British offensive had not resumed until February 1918, which was the first action after his arrival, and he must have taken part in it. The British took Kit and Khan al Baghdadi in March, and Kifri in April. These three towns are on the Tigris north of Baghdad. They were still short of Mosul, however, which, with its reported oil reserves, was a stated objective.

After the taking of Kifri, the British held up their advance and in October negotiations began (elsewhere) between the Allies and the Turks on armistice terms. While these were still going on, a War Office instruction was received in Mespot to the effect that "Every effort must be made to score on the Tigris before the final whistle blows". In response to this, a British force left Baghdad on 23rd October 1918. Within two days it covered 120 kilometres. A last engagement was fought, the Battle of Sharqat, resulting in the capture of almost the entire Ottoman Sixth Army. The impressive classical encircling movement which Bill had observed from his vantage point was quite probably this battle, the last of the war in

Mespot. A local armistice was signed following it, which the British immediately broke by continuing their advance towards Mosul in breach of its provisions, ignoring outraged Turkish protests. They marched unopposed into Mosul on 14th November 1918, three days after the armistice had put an end to the war in Europe.

It may have been that the Turks wisely realised that the war was all but over and that further loss of life was not justified. The savage fighting of the earlier years had lessened in ferocity by 1918. The Ottoman Empire was widely believed to be crumbling, and did not in fact long survive the war.

Bill waxed almost lyrical about the pleasure of fighting the Turks after the horrors of France. He referred to their chivalrous and "gentlemanly" conduct of hostilities. Exchanges of prisoners were regularly arranged. The Turkish commander insisted on maintaining good communications with his British counterpart. Messengers under a flag of truce were regularly received and dispatched to avoid the possibility of any unfortunate misunderstandings. One message (which was, admittedly, considered "a bit much") suggested that it was not chivalrous for the British to employ two artillery pieces when their opponents had only one!

Bill made a distinction between the opposing army and the native Bedouin Arabs. The Bedouin were, of course, the indigenous tribesmen over whose territory the two armies were fighting. They were on their home ground and knew the terrain perfectly, as well as how to cross it inconspicuously and silently – they could steal up on sentries and guards unseen, and remove rifles from apparently well-guarded stores without being detected. He spoke of them as something of a pest. In normal times the tribes ran their own affairs without either interference or assistance from the Ottoman Authorities.

The story of the Flooded Coalmine was one which Bill related to his

BRITISH TROOPS ENTER BAGHDAD.

eldest son, Paul, who recalls it as follows. The British Army realised that a coal mine existed in territory they had captured. Because they needed coal as fuel for the steam engines in their equipment, they decided to get the mine working. It had filled with water while unused, and all the coalfaces were underwater. It apparently needed to be drained continuously by pumping for output of coal to be possible. The Sappers set about getting the pumps working. These pumps were driven by steam engines –

A VILLAGE IN MESPOT

coal-fired steam engines. There was no remaining stock of coal at the mine, so it was necessary to bring in supplies. After some work the pumps were persuaded to function and the water level began to fall. As it fell, the consumption of coal required for pumping increased. Eventually, nevertheless, it was possible to begin working the coalfaces on a small scale and the mine became self-sufficient.

Considerable effort was required to keep up any output from it, and it became clear that the output of coal was only just equal to the consumption of coal for pumping. Eventually, after considerable expenditure of work and resources, the whole enterprise was abandoned as unproductive.

Bill began his repatriation to England very soon after armistice day, re-embarking at Basra, 700 km to the south, and sailing home using the same route as going out, eventually making port in Liverpool.

On the 14th May 1919 "Temporary Lieutenant W. P. Andrews M.C." is gazetted "to be acting Captain". At this stage of the war, these listings appear to have fallen far behind the actual events they record. The photograph in Mespot in 1917 shows him wearing Captain's insignia.

The gazette also records, on 19th April 1919, his "relinquishing his commission on completion of service". He once mentioned that he had briefly

BASRA, 1918. THE WAR IS OVER AND THE TROOPS ARE PREPARING TO BOARD SHIP FOR HOME.

reached Acting Major (two steps up from his "nominal" rank) by the end of the war, but that was not gazetted, perhaps because he left the service so soon after this.

The manner of Bill's leaving the British Army is notable. When his turn came for demobilisation, he was, to his delight, offered a commission in the regular (peace-time) army. This was a considerable compliment because only a tiny percentage of the huge wartime army was offered permanence. It was also a secure livelihood in a Britain where prospects of employment for demobilised soldiers were bleak. "The Land Fit for Heroes to Live In", which had been Lloyd George's slogan in an election during the closing stages of the war, was long quoted as the definitive broken electioneering pledge.

Bill awaited his first posting as a "regular" with the cheering prospect of a burgeoning military career before him. When the posting came, it was to Ireland. This sounded like a piece of great good fortune until he realised that he was to be part of an army being sent to Ireland to suppress the continuing unrest which followed the 1916 Rising and became the War of Independence. Bill immediately told his superiors it was impossible for him to undertake to fight against his own people; he could not accept the posting. It was pointed out to him that as a soldier he was obliged to obey orders; refusal of an order was mutiny, punishable as such; "orders is Orders". He replied that he would resign. This was true patriotism (to Ireland) because it was not a public gesture that would receive recognition, much less admiration. In the upshot his resignation was accepted.

THE OFFICERS IN MESPOT: BILL IS THE ONE SEATED ON THE RIGHT RELYING ON AN OVERSIZED PITH HELMET FOR HIS SAFETY.

The date for his demobilisation, 19th April 1919, marks the end of Bill's war. The taking of Mosul was on 14th November 1918, three days after the date of the Armistice in France. Starting on that date an army in the field, at Sharqat, had to be disengaged, transported to Basra and embarked there (assuming there were ships to board), and then sailed right around the Cape back to Liverpool. Following that Bill was offered the regular army commission and accepted it, given the posting to Ireland and refused it; then had his resignation accepted – all in five months.

He returned to civilian life and instantly lost the status of "war hero of Europe and Asia" to become "ex-soldier with a 50% disability" – unemployed and very glad of even the small disability pension.

CHAPTER 6

The Family Man

Once Bill had left the army he returned to working as a civil engineer as he had done before the war. But first, while in Cork, he was approached by "friends", the only identification he would ever divulge of them, with a request for a loan of his uniform for 2 or 3 days. They revealed that it was to be used in an operation to free a number of men who had been captured by the British in the struggle for Irish independence. They were being held "in Kilkenny", possibly Kilkenny gaol, but more likely a complete red herring to keep Bill from knowing any of the operational details. A British Army lorry, which had already been acquired, and a uniformed armed escort for the prisoners, would drive up to the prison, announce that they "had come to collect the IRA prisoners", load them up and drive away. The only thing they were short of was an officer's uniform.

BRITISH ARMY CROSSLEY LORRY, 1918.

Bill realised it could be a serious matter for him. If the scheme went wrong and his uniform was found it would certainly mean trouble for him – serious trouble – but that was not what held him back. He made it a condition before he agreed to it that there would be no bloodshed. He had served four years in the British Army. If he had not, reluctantly, refused a permanent commission he could now be on the opposite side. He would not aid a scheme that would involve killing his recent brothers-in-arms. He was assured that the essence of the scheme was to use deception, not force, and he heard enough to be convinced.

Uncle Bill's Tin Hat

BILL IN 1922, A PHOTOGRAPH
SENT TO CHRISTINA

In the event the ruse was completely successful. The lorry drove in through the gate, waved through by the prison guards who deferred to the uniform in the front seat, the prisoners were handed over in a calm and seemingly routine transfer and driven away to freedom.

This is a story which Bill told us as a matter not to be divulged to others. We feel free to tell it now, fifty years after his death. We have tried to find any record of it which would confirm or amplify his version, but have drawn a complete blank, to the extent that we were tempted to omit the story entirely. A story heard from Bill's own lips, however, is worth a place, even if it is only a story.

After leaving the army Bill "cut loose" for a while. It isn't hard to see why. Military discipline and the conventions of the officers' mess had controlled his behaviour for five years of his young adult life. Food and accommodation had been provided; he had been "under orders", the appropriate uniform specified for every occasion. He'd exerted the same discipline over others, been wounded, led men into danger and worked with them under fire, his life at risk several times a week. He had seen death at close quarters more than once and had proved just slippery enough to escape its clutches. At the end of it all he found himself turned out to restart life as a civilian along with a million other ex-servicemen all competing for employment that would stretch to only a small fraction.

He had one hard-bought quittance: in exchange for losing half a lung and incurring the disease that would eventually end his life, he had a lieutenant's 50 per cent disability pension. There must have been times when it saved him from starvation.

The realisation that the war really was over after those astonishing, indescribable years and – outstandingly – that he was one of the lucky few to have survived; that must have been the most deeply felt emotion. Perhaps not mentioned or even given conscious thought, it was nevertheless the abiding fact of life. Memories of incidents in the war and the men who shared them inevitably included thoughts of those who had not. Difficult and unwelcoming as his return to civilian life had been, it was a life which he had been very close to being denied.

Survived he had, though.

Now what?

Who could blame him for celebrating survival and freedom with any companions who'd match him round for round? Ex-servicemen learnt quickly that there was no one who could understand their war experiences, neither civilian nor even fellow soldier, neither relative nor stranger; their fearsome experiences were theirs alone and were both unforgettable and indescribable. What a man could do was to get together with any one who would make a drinking companion. The most searing and harrowing experiences of their lives now belonged in another time and place. Life would be safer now, more comfortable and, inevitably, duller. Just one occasion is all that Bill recounted later of his post-war shenanigans, on the way from club to car.

Bill: "Here's your car. Can you manage to drive? You're staggering."

Car owner (pronouncing carefully): "I can drive when I can't walk."

Bill's next memory was waking up in hospital with his right arm in plaster. He had to master, as quickly as possible, writing with his left hand to keep the precious job he happened to have at the time.

If he was irresponsible, he was not as reckless of life as the army command had been at the Somme. Millions of survivors were similarly trying to forget memories of the war, to forget how their lives had been diced with recklessly, time after time, each time increasing their risk of death.

This experience had an effect on Bill's personality in later life: "That looks a bit risky" was not how he would judge a situation; he weighed his risks and his decisions were calculated, not reckless, *but when he saw an opportunity he grasped it enthusiastically.*

He became a jovial, agreeable, definite young man: "quick" is the word that leaps to mind. He walked quickly and thought quickly. His talk was direct and simple, problems were dealt with "on the hoof". He had put the horrors of war behind him and command of his unit had given him an easy authority. His brushes with death had been close but he had survived them all. He didn't profess optimism as a creed, he just felt lucky. He knew the need to enjoy life for the while he possessed it. He had a sense of fun and a stock of funny stories, seldom mentioning the war.

CHRISTINA MCALEER, 1922.

Bill had to be ready to "follow the work" over a wide swathe of Britain and Ireland: he mentioned Dublin, Belfast, Scotland and the North of England as places he worked in. The incident with the broken arm took place in England. His sensible, considerably older brother, Michael, was working in the Board of Works in London – he was non-combatant and barely affected by the war. Charming, extremely cautious and somewhat unimaginative, he found Bill's wild behaviour as baffling as his war experiences. It was Michael who brought Bill to the Hughes' house in London; the Hughes were a prosperous, property-owning family in Omagh. Their house in London seems to have been a very hospitable one for anyone from, or connected with, their old home town. Michael had visited them – and had met Christina there.

She was a high-achiever in her own right. Her early life had been linked with Bill's family during their early years in Omagh. She had won a job in the civil service in London by scoring well above the "cut off" in the first exam for recruitment of women, making her something of a phenomenon in Omagh at the time.

That success meant that from living in Omagh for her whole life to that date and seldom leaving it, she moved immediately to the metropolis of London to take up a job which, although she found it "undemanding" – read boring – would have been considered highly prestigious for a man; for a young woman it was (a) non-existent until that time and (b) demanding of the highest standards associated with London, the capital city of the whole, vast British Empire.

She was a seasoned traveller by boat and train between London and Omagh, taking the mail boat from Holyhead to DunLaoghaire. She recounted how, on one crossing to Ireland, there was a noticeable group of five or six formally dressed Irish men aboard. Men, travelling as a party, often establish a bonhomie and jollity among themselves, but there was no trace of that in this group. Sadness was their characteristic mood, a terrible sadness. She was witnessing one of the most significant events in Irish history. The group was the Irish delegation to talks in London, the hero Michael Collins among them, who had been sent with full plenipotentiary powers from the Dáil to negotiate and to sign a treaty. This they had just done, bringing about, at a stroke, the end of British rule from Dublin and of the Irish War of Independence. But they had been intimidated and isolated in London and had not been able to avoid signing a treaty which partitioned Ireland into a mainly Catholic Republic and Protestant North. For this they faced a harsh judgement at home.

When the ship reached DunLaoghaire there was a huge crowd of their supporters on the quay to welcome the delegation and cheer them to the echo.

Successful revolutions notoriously devour their young. Over the years

Christina had cause to remember their terrible sadness as, one by one, those delegates met their deaths at the hands of fellow Irishmen, opponents of the treaty.

When she met Bill she had been working in London for seven years, from 1915 to 1922. Michael (40 or so years later) divulged to Christina's children that he had "had an eye on her for himself" before Bill's arrival. The younger brother, ex-officer, war-veteran, closer in age to the girl and with a much more vibrant personality, swept him aside. The perspicacious Christina did not find it difficult to read his character. Her judgement was distinctly favourable.

It was in 1922 that they met in the London suburb. They were married in Omagh on 23rd April 1924.

BILL AND CHRISTINA.

By her own account she had not the least regret in abandoning that career and marrying him. "Matrimony is the best career," she often repeated, particularly when her daughter was considering her own future after finishing school.

Christina's wedding was the sort of glamorous and happy occasion that girls dream of. Back in Omagh, Bill was honoured as a recent war-hero and commissioned officer and current successful professional when those three accomplishments were not at all common among the Catholic population. Although, in all likelihood, he had not seen Omagh since

The Family Man

THE WEDDING PHOTO: NOT A SINGLE MEMBER OF BILL'S FAMILY CROSSED THE BORDER TO ATTEND.

leaving it as a schoolboy, both he and his parents were well remembered; now he and his bride were a native son and daughter who had both made good in the wide world and returned to town to marry. They seem to have been determined to put on a show for the relatives back home, which they, in turn, were happy to enjoy without resentment.

The anomaly that his wedding was not attended by Bill's father or any of his siblings was something he never explained. The photographs show Christina's family in their wedding finery with the clergy attending, but not even one member of Bill's family. Christina's family suspected that this was an intended slight, that the Andrews clan was claiming to out-rank them socially. The McAleers were, in fact, a family of considerable standing in Omagh. They were "comfortable" and occupied an established, prestigious position in the town.

Those sisters of Bill's, who didn't attend, had floated free from their origins and had decided that they should first find themselves husbands and then proceed to become "matrons of Dublin society". These plans occupied all their attention; Omagh was an irrelevancy. That the Border was a recent creation constituted an uncertainty and an excuse, if a somewhat specious one, not to go. They were not concerned that their absence might be seen as a slight, they had other fish to fry. Bill's mother, who might have pressed them to attend, had died seven years earlier. Sisters and father stayed home.

If there was a snub intended, it didn't affect Bill's dealings with his sisters as they were all sociable and welcoming in later times whenever they happened to be in the same town. Christina, however, always had a defensive cone around her where the sisters were concerned, mistrusting their motives and fearing their unpredictability. Her way of defending her pride was to let it be known that she, on her own, had produced more children than all four of them together.

CHRISTINA AND BILL ON THEIR WEDDING DAY.

The Family Man

The wedding was carried off with panache. A photograph of the groom and best man shows them dressed to the nines, relaxed, confident and brimming with bonhomie. The bride's dress (in royal blue) was created for her by a couturier named de Moncho, a friend of Bill's. Christina had been given a substantial lump sum payment on leaving her post in the civil service and she had, characteristically, blown it all on her wedding gown. In local parlance, "Omey'd never seen the like."

Their first born, a daughter whom they named Joan, was born 16 months later, followed by three brothers. These were years of hard graft for Bill. The limited duration of civil-engineering contracts meant repeated episodes of seeking new work. Very often that meant a change of location as well. Christina kept count of the times she set up family homes. During Bill's lifetime the number topped thirty.

In February 1927, Bill's father died in Dublin. Bill was with him at the time.

BILL'S FATHER WILLIAM DIED IN 1927. BILL AND FAMILY WERE LIVING IN RATHFARNHAM AT THE TIME AND BILL WAS WITH HIM WHEN HE DIED.

Also in early 1927, at the time of the birth of the second of his children, Paul, Bill suffered a recurrence of his lung problems. He realised that he was seriously ill and needed specialist attention. He found a lung specialist on Harley Street who advised that it was 'flu requiring bed-rest and aspirins! He was then fortunate enough to encounter an Irish doctor in London, who realised that he had a collapsed lung, got him to Dublin and into The Mater, one of the city's leading hospitals, where he was brought back to health. The befriending doctor (whose name, Harbison, is all we know about him), realising that Bill just didn't have the resources to pay his fee as well as hospital fees and the expenses associated with his first son's birth, told Bill his birthday present for the new-born was to forego any fee for treatment.

It was possibly on this visit to Dublin that Bill, once more at the end of an assignment, applied for a job as an agricultural inspector, a job for

GROWING FAMILY, 1938. FROM LEFT: PAUL, CHRISTINA, MICHAEL, JOAN AND JOHN.

which he had neither qualifications nor relevant experience. His degree and commission in the army must have been enough to get him shortlisted for interview.

He decided to be quite honest at the interview; he explained to the board that he had applied because he was desperately in need of a job; his wife had just had a baby and he was actually unemployed although he had been working until not long before. He gained the board's sympathy. They accepted his application at face value and proceeded with the interview. One member, though, decided to ask at least one extremely relevant question relating to the job's duties. If Bill were inspecting a farm to check on a claim that a particular crop was being grown on stated acreage, would he be able to identify the crop on each field? Could he, for instance, describe the difference between two named varieties of wheat? Bill could not claim to have this expertise. What, then, he was asked, would he do

BILL WITH HIS 16 H.P. AUSTIN AT LYTHAM-ST.ANNE'S.

in those circumstances? He replied that he would make inquiries from neighbouring farmers. He didn't get the job, and there followed another return to England, a near-penniless one at that. These must have been tough times for him and Christina. He, and that growing family, had to be willing to traverse Britain and Ireland widely and quickly to take up jobs where and when they became available, to keep a salary coming in. There were jobs in Lancashire, in Yorkshire, Belfast and various other locations.

Christina had learnt the piano as a child and it was always a pleasure for her to have a piano to play. At one time she and the family had accommodation in a house with other occupants. One of these, close-by, she could hear practising the piano during the day. She listened to this stranger's playing but – at first – could make nothing of the kind of classical music he was playing. One particular piece, which he worked on incessantly, baffled her utterly. After many hearings she began to make some sense of it and there came a day when she grasped its meaning. She grew to appreciate its subtleties and enjoy hearing it. She had no idea of its composer or origin. She told this story herself. She didn't say by what means or through what agency, but she did eventually discover its title and said "it was worth listening out for."

Uncle Bill's Tin Hat

This could be seen as a romantic situation: a young woman, talented and cultured, newly arrived and isolated in some drab Lancashire town, gradually becoming enraptured with music written, it turned out, by a Spanish composer of the romantic period. One cannot help wondering what her attitude might have been to the invisible player whom she knew only from his playing. The piece? Not very well known, it was called 'Seguidillas'. It comes from a suite: Cantos De Espana by Albeniz, a nineteenth century Spanish composer.

Christina didn't spend all her days in those early married years sighing over invisible piano players, if it even came to that. She did, of course, soon have babies and then toddlers to occupy her as well. Another skill, at some time later, shows her in a much more twentieth-century and proactive mode. She attended furniture auctions and bid at them.

THE CAR ON HOLIDAY TO KNOKKE-LE-ZOUTE, BELGIUM, 1938 WHERE THE ANDREWS CLAN STAYED IN THE HOTEL DU FAMILLE.

There were several reasons why auctions at this time should offer exceptional opportunities. The first reason was that the old British "landed gentry" were being bankrupted by huge, and increasing, taxes. The contents of their grand houses were "coming under the hammer". Simultaneously, the cotton trade, which had been a source of enormous wealth in the North of England, had been wiped out by production in India. This, too, caused the contents of homes that had been lavishly furnished with cotton money to be sold off.

The supply was ample and included wonderful items, while the demand wasn't. For a bright young wife, whose resourceful husband was beginning to make his way in the world, it was a wonderful opportunity to furnish with some style. She did not look this gift horse in the mouth.

Bill's status as a civil engineer was improving, and his natural motivation, never lacking, was augmented by the needs of his family. Now his income had begun to pick up. Early in the 1930s he joined the firm in which he was to make his career for the remainder of his working life barring wartime: The Cement and Concrete Association.

REMEMBERING WWI AT ARMENTIÈRES IN NORTHERN FRANCE WHILE ON HOLIDAY IN BELGIUM.

That company and he proved a good fit; it provided an outlet for his multiple and diverse talents and he became a valued staff member. In 1936 he was selected for a well-paid job at the head office in Victoria, Central London.

Another less happy episode, but one which also hints at improved financial circumstances, occurred in 1935; it concerned Paul, Bill's eldest son. He was at a Christian Brothers' day school near Liverpool but was obviously finding the school impossible. He and the Brothers just did not get on together. Bill, remembering a wartime friendship he had had with a chaplain, a Benedictine monk whose monastery ran a boarding school, packed the unfortunate Paul off there, at nine years of age. The school was called Belmont Abbey, no longer extant. This action does not bespeak a straitened budget.

ANOTHER FAMILY CAR.

The results, however, were disastrous not only for pupil but, more surprisingly, for that school as well! To say that the school did not suit the boy is to gloss over a myriad; but Paul had the compensating satisfaction of shutting it down in mid-term, before it was agreed that it was not right for him.

He did this by infecting the school (twice) with Diphtheria. He was unwittingly carrying the bacteria all-but undetectably in his nose. Swabbing of his throat showed him apparently uninfected and it was this that allowed him to carry out a repeat infection. His game attempt to cause a second shut-down was thwarted only by the imminence of the end of term. Bill's family moved from Liverpool to Wimbledon while these episodes played out and the monks' enthusiasm for this student waned, in spite of his considerable intellectual ability.

He moved school again to Wimbledon College, a Jesuit-run day school

The Family Man

where he thrived mightily. By 1939 he had been joined there by his two brothers, the younger of whom did not leave it finally until 1951.

A leafy area of Wimbledon, home of the All-English Lawn Tennis and Croquet Club, was the location of the substantial house that Bill rented for his family when he started work in London. The couple seem to have hit Wimbledon, and the 1936 Irish community in London, like a tidal wave of energy and enthusiasm. Before they left just four years later, they had become leading figures in the National University of Ireland (NUI) Club, the Irish Literary Society, the Institution of Civil Engineers, the Catenian Association; they were prominent in Wimbledon Parish, run by the Jesuits. The bringing up of four lively children seems to have been used as an asset rather than a hindrance to their social activities.

As an instance of their standing, the Papal Nuncio, Cardinal Godfrey (whose Nunciature was located in Wimbledon) was a friend who frequently visited the house. This all represents an extraordinary contrast to the status of the young engineer a few years earlier, moving from job to job with bleak spells of unemployment.

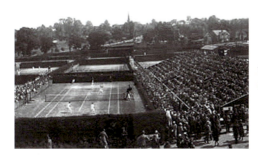

WIMBLEDON 1938.

The end of the idyll in Wimbledon was brought about by a little Austrian with a tiny moustache: Adolf Hitler, Führer of Germany.

Bill and his family were aware of Herr Hitler's activities long before the start of the war. Sponsored by his firm, Bill was one of a party of roads engineers from England invited to visit Germany to inspect the autobahnen, the world's first motorways. "Inspect", they would have said; "Admire", was what their hosts had in mind. As it happened this visit took place in 1938, which was the year of the Munich Crisis, brought about by the same Austrian's threat to "annexe the Sudetenland" to Germany. This was a formerly German and still largely German-speaking region, which had been included in the newly-created state of Czechoslovakia by the Versailles treaty after WWI. Britain and France had

BRITISH ROADS ENGINEERS AT SAN SOUCI, POTSDAM, 1938.

guaranteed the integrity of the Czech boundaries. The guarantee committed them to defend the territory if the Germans should attempt to usurp it.

As history recalls, Chamberlain, the British prime minister, flew to Germany to avert the crisis. (He did avert it, temporarily, by reneging on the guarantee and abandoning the Czechs to their fate at the hands of the Germans.) War was prevented, or rather postponed. The Andrews family rejoiced because Bill's visit to Germany coincided with the crisis which threatened an immediate outbreak of war. If war had broken out he could well have been interned in Germany, as an enemy alien, for its duration. He recounted how the attitude of the German engineers, who were their hosts, switched from great affability to utter frigidity and back to even greater conviviality as the crisis evolved.

And he did admire, as his hosts doubtless intended, not only the technical and organisational achievement of the motorways, but, even more notable, the tremendously high morale of the workers and their patriotic pride in their work. He was a naturally affable man and thoroughly enjoyed the experience.

Bill's Irish nationality had somehow become known to the Germans.

The Family Man

THE DELEGATION LUNCHING AT THE AUTOBAHN LABOUR CAMP IN POTSDAM.

He had an exchange with one of his hosts at the time of the Crisis. Part of the German case for the return of the Sudetenland was that the large German population there was being discriminated against and generally ill-treated under the Czech regime. Bill asked this English-speaking host if it was really true that the Sudeten Germans were badly treated. "Mr Andrews, they are treating our people worse than the British ever treated your people in Ireland!" Bill was impressed that a German engineer knew enough of Irish history for such a comparison to occur to him.

The Helmet and the savage damage it incurred are testimony to the ruthless ferocity with which the first war had been fought by the armies of these hosts and these guests; armies in which many of those hosts and guests had themselves fought – as had Bill, of course. That mindless ferocity makes a telling contrast to the affability and friendly admiration that were blossoming in peacetime.

THE INSTITUTE OF CIVIL ENGINEERS OF LONDON DELEGATION BUS ON THE MODERN ENGINEERING MARVEL OF 1938, THE AUTOBAHN.

After 1938 and the Munich Crisis, Germany occupied first the Sudetenland and then the whole of Czechoslovakia. Next she invaded Poland and this precipitated World War II in September 1939.

Chapter 7

World War II

At the beginning of World War II Bill volunteered once more for the Sappers while Christina and the children, Joan, Paul, John and Michael, now aged from 14 to 7, fled from London to Omagh.

Germany had invaded Poland and blitzed Warsaw with a sudden and intense bombing of the city by the Luftwaffe. This was the second blitz that had ever happened. The first, at Guernica in Spain, had also been carried out by German bombers fighting at that time for Franco during the Spanish civil war.

A BOMBER OVER LONDON.

Poland succumbed and France was soon forced to surrender after a lightning German defeat of the combined French and British armies. The Germans achieved in a few short months what they had failed to do in the whole of World War I: they occupied northern France right up to the Channel. This meant that the Luftwaffe had the use of airfields for a blitz on London which was in easy range. German heavy artillery was brought up to the Channel where they could see the British coast across the Straits of Dover and started shelling the southern coast of England.

Christina had lived in London during the first war when there had been desultory air raids by zeppelins, nothing like a World War II blitz but still to be feared and evaded. Now, from the house in Wimbledon, in the quiet hours of the night, the sound of the cross-channel bombardment

CHILDREN BEING EVACUATED FROM LONDON.

reminded her of those days and she quickly made up her mind to whisk the children away from London. At the same time the British Government was organising the wholesale evacuation of all children from the capital. Omagh, Christina's birthplace, and where all her siblings lived, was where her thoughts automatically turned to as a place of refuge. Serendipitously, it is as remote from Dover and those French airfields as almost any part of Britain or Ireland.

This move would put them at a comforting distance from that source of danger, but it meant leaving Bill behind. To pay rent on two houses was

THE LONDON BLITZ.

out of the question, so the lease of the leafy house in Wimbledon would have to be surrendered.

There then occurred an encounter, which seems typical of many at turning points of Bill's life. In 1940, quite accidentally, he ran into a Brigadier Luby on Victoria Street who had been his commanding officer in France during World War I.

"Andrews! Just the sort of man I'm desperate for! We're getting up an expedition to Egypt. Can't get enough Sapper officers. An experienced officer like yourself would be absolutely invaluable."

There and then, over coffee, Luby invited Bill to re-join the Sappers with the immediate rank of lieutenant colonel, and early promotion to full colonel. To do so he would have to re-enlist. Although he was now well over the age at which he could have been conscripted, he would be warmly welcomed back as a volunteer.

Bill volunteered.

THE BRODIE HELMET GETS A NEW USE IN WORLD WAR II.

Uncle Bill's Tin Hat

LONDON 1940.

In spite of his joining up "for Egypt", Northern Ireland was where Bill, too, spent the war. An army medical inspection found him "unfit for active service". This was something that neither he nor Luby had anticipated. Egypt was an active-service expedition. He may well have challenged the medical finding, but he had been receiving a 50 per cent disability pension from the War Office since 1919. He was 45, his lungs

THE BLITZ.

World War II

were damaged and he actually was unfit for active service, his campaign in Mespot 20 years earlier notwithstanding.

So, while his family made a new home at his birthplace, Bill was still in London and felt the brunt of the Blitz, as feared, as soon as his family had fled. It did not seem to faze him in the least; he recounted it with zest, verging on enthusiasm. Before the lease was up, Bill slept at the family house in Wimbledon under the dining table for protection and at one time he was woken by a massive explosion, a bomb taking out the house next door. He walked away unharmed.

Once the Sappers had enlisted Bill, they held on to him; they had camps to build all over Britain and Northern Ireland and an experienced officer who was also a practicing civil engineer was too good to part with. He was offered a choice of location and was assigned to his first choice, the Northern Ireland Command. Luby's promises of promotion did not apply away from his Egypt force so Bill started World War II as a major, but he soon secured promotion to Lieutenant Colonel (Lt Col), a notch up from major.

BELFAST 1940.

He was posted to Belfast on his arrival in Northern Ireland and was staying in a hotel near the centre when he heard once again the familiar growl of German bombers. There were two or three raids over a period of about a week. He was appointed Air Raid Warden for the hotel and made arrangements for the safety of the other guests. He seemed more stimulated than frightened. He joked that Hitler's bombers were aware of his movements and followed him with the air raids. He would have been flattered more than worried if that had been true.

Uncle Bill's Tin Hat

One of the guests in the hotel refused to go to the cellar which was designated as the air-raid shelter. Bill went to the man's room to see if it could be a safe place. The bed was right in front of the window. If there were an explosion outside, the bed and its occupant would be riddled with splinters of glass. Bill explained this to the recalcitrant occupant. He replied, contemptuously, that there were sound wooden shutters he would put across. Bill knew that was no protection and he had to use his authority as Air Warden to get the guest, however reluctant and sceptical, to join the others in the cellar when the sirens sounded. The bombs came close and after the "All Clear" they returned to the room to see what had happened. It was as if Bill had arranged his own vindication. The heavy shutters which had been drawn, had been blown in and come down squarely across the bed. They, and the whole room, were littered with debris and broken glass. Bill enjoyed retelling that story.

In the meantime Christina and the children landed in Omagh. Their Wimbledon idyll was over and gone forever. Christina mourned it for years. This was a shattering change in her status which happened almost overnight.

First there was the harrowing voyage by train and mailboat to Northern Ireland. They decided to keep the boat journey as short as possible as it was exposed to attack from U-boats: this meant an all-day train journey all the way to Stranraer, near Ayr in Scotland. They transferred to the mailboat on the quay, the children lugging suitcases and boxes, Christina organising a porter for the trunks. Then they had the sickening crossing of the wild North Channel to Belfast and finally the long, slow train journey to Omagh.

One day the family was well respected in Wimbledon, occupying a modern, comfortable suburban house with a maid in attendance. Following two days of harrowing travel, Christina had been reduced to something verging on refugee status. She arrived in Omagh with four young children, all under 15 years of age, without any accommodation and with only the possessions they had brought with them, now dependent for accommodation on the charity of her relatives.

It had been her decision to take her children away from London and wait out the war in Omagh. The house in which she had grown up, the house above the pub, McAleer's Campsie Bar at the end of the town, was still occupied by her siblings, her brother Charlie, and two unmarried sisters. Charlie was already married and had one child, still an infant; the

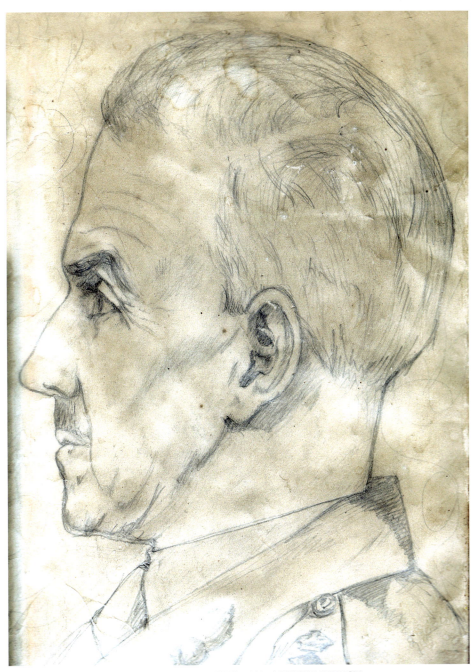

LT.-COL. W. P. ANDREWS, 1941, A PENCIL SKETCH
BY HIS DAUGHTER, JOAN, THEN AGED 15.

STRULE VIEW, THEIR FIRST HOUSE IN OMAGH, RIGHT BESIDE THE OLD GAOL ARCH.

house was well filled. The situation was seen as an emergency, Christina and four schoolchildren, arriving fatherless, were squeezed in somehow, sleeping in shared rooms and shared beds. It was a crush and this dictated the urgent need to find other accommodation.

Christina was resourceful and intelligent, but because Bill had always handled the renting of houses she was entirely new to the formalities involved. She had to master them quickly.

Her brother Charlie was a brisk businessman and he knew everything going on in the town. He had inherited the bar – and considerable business ability – from his father. He exerted himself to help Christina get settled. The only accommodation available that was even nearly adequate was a house which, by a wry coincidence, was part of the gaol buildings in which Bill was born and had lived as a child. It was large enough to house the family, so, to meet the immediate need for a home, Christina took it. The only provision for cooking was a "Black Stove" – a fire had to be lit in it and the oven given time to heat up. There was no gas connection although it did have electricity.

It was unfurnished, so Christina had to cadge enough furniture from her siblings to make it habitable until her own things could be taken out

World War II

of storage in Wimbledon. Looking back, what impresses her children even to the present day is how soon it was that they had a home again.

The absence of Bill transformed what had been a conventional two-parent family into something different. Without Bill's dominant presence, the family environment became less demanding; feminine influence was stronger. Their new little house was safe, cosy and ran smoothly. It was home.

LISSANELLY, THEIR SECOND HOUSE IN OMAGH.

A piece of family lore from the first days in that house: a clatter at the front door was answered by Joan, 14 years old. A big man in working clothes looked at her and asked "Uz shiunn?" Joan was baffled. He caught her gaze and spoke more insistently, "Uz Shiunn?" Drawing another blank he cried once more "Uz Shi-UNN?" Joan backed away from him and reported to her mother. "A big man who keeps on saying the same thing that I can't understand." Christina went to the door and bought some logs from him; he was calling house to house selling them. Joan still didn't know what he had been saying to her. The strongest version of the Tyrone accent used to darken "i"s to a sound like the "u" in "duck". Simply, he was asking "Is she in?"

BILL'S FOUR CHILDREN DURING THE WAR: MICHAEL, JOAN, PAUL AND JOHN.

This incident, perhaps because it was a perfect example of the sort of small problems the children had in adjusting from Wimbledon to Omagh, became a source of huge hilarity. Even 70 years later it can still set off fits of giggling.

The tenor of the household was very different from the way it had been in Wimbledon. Without the school friends they had left behind, the children turned more to one another and became more close-knit. They had arrived in Omagh in the spring and didn't start school again until the start of the next school year in September, giving them four months of freedom. There are memories of some quite cultured activities; trying to sing songs in harmony, producing a "concert" with an original "play" and recitations. There was a tennis club that they joined in Omagh – it was very difficult to get equipment or even tennis balls "because of the war".

Reaching these adjustments involved difficulties, even fights and some rebelliousness among the boys. Christina coped with these in Bill's absence. Then the family was again split up as a result of Paul's allergy to the Christian Brothers who ran the only Catholic boys' school in Omagh, the same one Bill had attended forty years earlier. Paul and The Brothers were spared another encounter; he was booked into the nearest boarding school, thirty miles away in Derry, while his two younger brothers enrolled in their father's old school. Joan was sent to the Loreto convent school where her mother's scholastic achievements were still remembered.

World War II

Of course when Bill finally arrived everything had to change. The small house and, in particular, the fact that it was cheek-to-jowl with his Omagh Gaol birthplace, seemed to cause him embarrassment rather than pleasure. He and Christina had one of their few real arguments, whispering on into the night while the children tried to sleep. Christina was bitterly vexed that he was castigating her efforts in setting up home and scoffing at her family's generous help.

Bill got his way and he found them a fine house in grounds of its own on the outskirts and moved Joan, Paul and John to prestigious schools in Dublin while Michael remained at home.

Bill's promotion to Lt Col was of significance because it gave him an independent area inside which all Sapper services came under his control. He had attained the significant role of "CRE" (Commander Royal Engineers). It was an appointment of some consequence in the Sappers and enjoyed considerable status and authority. Bill was quite at ease with that.

CHRISTINA AND CHILDREN RELAXING IN THE HAY.

As CRE, he was assigned a staff car and a driver, a big Humber with khaki paintwork. He was not permitted to take the wheel himself, not having been to Army Driving School, so he was given a driver from the ATS, the army's separate woman's corps. She was an army-trained driver and she remained his driver for several years. It was an arrangement that Christina viewed with mild suspicion.

Shortly after he arrived in Northern Ireland, an acute shortage of engineers was curtailing the work of the Sappers, building camps for trainee troops. There was little chance of getting qualified engineers in Great Britain where they were subject to recruitment like every other young man, immediately on graduation. Bill saw a possibility of getting his old college in Cork to supply the need. Construction had slowed sharply in Ireland and their graduates were facing unemployment. He contacted the professor in his old college and soon a cohort of enthusiastic young engineers crossed the border to fill the civilian vacancies. They were handpicked and they proved eminently successful. Their appointment

BUILDING A NISSEN HUT.

was accomplished with the speed required rather than the formalities laid down. Without Bill's role there would have been no chance of attracting them. Even when they knew of the vacancies, they were reluctant to work for the British Army in Northern Ireland and Bill's example and reassurance were crucial to convince them that it was not a betrayal of their country to do so.

This is a characteristic example of Bill's readiness to employ his enterprise whenever the opportunity arose rather than meekly following the rulebook.

Soon American troops were arriving as the first temporary residents in the camps. They came in two separate waves, the first, in 1941 - 42, for the invasion of North Africa, and the second, in 1944, for the "D-Day" invasion of mainland Europe.

Although the camps were built and prepared for the Americans, they were constructed to British Army standards and, of course, were completed before the Americans actually arrived. The British Army's accommodation was frugal even by British civilian standards. The arriving American military found it totally and utterly inadequate. This led to resentment on the British side that the Yanks wanted higher standards for their GIs than the British gave their Tommies.

A NISSEN HUT ENCAMPMENT.

The soft, moist weather of Northern Ireland made the situation worse: their trucks were heavier and more numerous than the roads in the camps could cope with. They ran the trucks onto the grass which rapidly churned into mud and in short order whole camps deteriorated into muddy quagmires. Winter was still to come.

While there was a basic goodwill between the Allies, there was strong rivalry between the Tommies and the Yanks and the issue of camp conditions became a serious one. The Americans needed someone to whom they could relate and who could produce some action on their problems and they found him in Lt Col Andrews. As well as not being English, he was a "proper soldier", a man who had seen combat, rather than "a civilian dressed in uniform". Bill managed to satisfy the living requirements of the Americans and he also formed many friendships among the American officers he dealt with. In the Sappers, Bill became known as A Man Who Could Talk to the Yanks and Keep Them Happy. The Andrews household became a hospitable spot for American officers, Fr. English, a chaplain from Chicago, a particular favourite.

Bill's immediacy in his approach to these problems was appreciated by the Americans. It was what they were used to. He promptly visited the site of complaints to see the situation himself; he didn't Request Written Reports nor Insist on Correct Channels of Communication. His easy touch was quite the exception in the early days of the American presence.

AMERICAN ARMY CHAPLAINS FR. ENGLISH AND FR. O'CONNOR AT THE CHAPEL.

In contrast, his wartime style of command with his own subordinates reverted to the style which had won him high regard in World War I. It was a military, no-nonsense, authoritarian style, quite different from a civilian work situation. The graduate engineers he recruited straight from university did not always find it a smooth ride. As late as the 1960s, one of those men, contacted in Dublin, was notably still smarting from the ferocity with which Bill had driven them. It did not make matters any easier for them that this was their first experience of paid employment after three years at college and that their work bore little relation to anything they had studied.

Bill had a notebook. It wouldn't have fitted in the pocket of a civilian suit, but uniform pockets were bigger. It was hard-back, bound at the top, opened up-and-over, with lined pages, a rubber band to keep it closed in his pocket, and it terrified his staff. It was where he recorded their orders and commitments from one visit to the next.

One evening he dropped in to Omagh in time for tea. He had a

World War II

A STANDARD NISSEN HUT: BILL'S COMPANY BUILT HUNDREDS OF THESE TO HOUSE THE TROOPS.

member of his staff with him. This was a mild, slightly portly, agreeable fellow. Christina chatted to him over tea. She made some reference to what Bill was like to work for and the man referred to the Notebook and how no-one wanted to see it coming out. Bill was amused. "Oh yes, my notebook. Always in my pocket. Even now. Look, here it is." He started to reach for his pocket but Christina, always conscious of a guest's comfort, intervened. Her voice took on a note of urgency, "No, dear! Not at tea. You're upsetting Mr Browett." The man's face had paled at the prospect of even a glimpse.

As more army camps were built there, Northern Ireland was divided into smaller pieces or "areas", each commanded by a CRE. At one time Bill's "area" was one based in Omagh and this was the only time that he could live at home during the war.

Here Bill built a Catholic chapel in the large British Army camp near the town. The chapel was needed for the Catholic chaplain who tended the garrison, which included a high proportion of the Catholics. The camp was a recruitment depot and many men from Éire, mostly Catholics, crossed the border to join up there. Bill was enthusiastic about the creation of this little chapel, seeing it as tying in with his faith. He lavished care and attention on it. It was not an impressive building externally, just an enlarged version of the standard Nissen Hut; but, inside, it had been remarkably transformed into a peaceful and devotional haven.

Bill wore his uniform in public with deft disregard for the sensitivities of both sides of the religious divide. He would attend Mass in the large Catholic church in Omagh dressed in his British Army Colonel's uniform and then cross the street to the County Club where no Catholic had ever come through their door and call for whiskey with his fellow-officers. His uniform ensured grudging compliance. He would pass an hour in the Club before retiring home for the Sunday lunch.

Uncle Bill's Tin Hat

He often told of occasions when his name, William, deceived the unwary about his religious affiliation. The army camps he was busy constructing were often built on large country estates sequestrated for the war effort and their grand houses were taken over by the officers as their own private clubs. Here he would drink his favourite whiskey into the evening with officers who knew him not as well as they might like to think. The conversation tended towards condemnation of the "Taigues" and "Papists" while Bill bided his time. Towards the end of the evening he stood up, straightened his tunic and announced that he had to leave as he had early Mass in the morning.

THE CHAPEL IN A NISSEN HUT, BUILT BY BILL, WHICH SO OFFENDED THE B-SPECIALS.

He often enjoyed recounting the result of this announcement, the blank amazement, the shuffling embarrassment, the wry grins from those who knew him best.

Northern Ireland at this time was assertively "A Protestant State for a Protestant people". There was an element in the Protestant community paranoid in its determination to ensure that the Catholic, nationalist population should be kept in a state of suppression. In Omagh this element found it a scandal that anyone from the suspect Catholic community should obtain such a prominent, influential and prestigious position as Bill held. It did not make it any easier for them to accept him that it was in the British Army that he had acquired prominence. They saw the army as protection from invasion by the real enemy, Éire across the border; the war in Europe was relatively remote and irrelevant. The building of a Catholic place of worship inside "their" army's camp was totally anathema to them.

> **Built Army Chapel**
>
> FOR his services to American troops in Northern Ireland during the war, Lt.-Col. W. P. Andrews, MC, a Catholic, was presented on Tuesday at the American Embassy with the USA Bronze Star Medal and citation.
>
> Col. Andrews was Commander Royal Engineers. At the infantry training centre in Omagh he built a Catholic chapel which was blessed and opened by Bishop Farren of Derry.
>
> Col. Andrews, now in civilian life, won his MC in the first World War.
>
> **'Guam Exiles' a myth**
>
> BISHOP BAUMGARTNER, OFMCap. Guam's Vicar

POST-WAR PUBLICITY FOR THE "CHAPEL" AND ITS CREATOR

If the "Roman" chapel at the camp had produced indignation, when it became known that the same upstart who was responsible for that outrage had also been arranging for men from the "enemy territory" across the border to be fixed up with well-paid jobs in the British Army's organisation, their rancour had to find an outlet. They decided to alert the unwary British military of the danger in which they were placing the United Kingdom.

They didn't get far.

They made an approach to Army Headquarters in Belfast using the "B Specials" as a channel. These were an auxiliary part-time reserve to the police in Northern Ireland and a notoriously sectarian body. During the war they were given the role that the Home Guard had in Britain, including its anti-espionage element. It was this role that they invoked when they presented evidence that Colonel Andrews was a disaffected anti-partitionist motivated by a desire to undermine British Army morale. They quoted his dark misdeeds – building a "Roman" place of worship inside Omagh Barracks, and introducing employees, who could well access classified intelligence, from Axis-sympathetic Éire across the border. They

Uncle Bill's Tin Hat

even complained that he was encouraging US Army recruits to drink in his brother-in-law's licensed premises in Omagh. Bill was shown the dossier they produced and also the response from the Army's security

B-SPECIALS.

service. The indictment was dismissed as unimpressive, unconvincing and largely concerned with matters which did not bear on wartime security. The army's enquiries that followed its reception had been straightforward and sensible, concluding that nothing in the accusations warranted any further action. A ringing endorsement of Bill's ability and enthusiasm was included in the response. His boss did not want to lose him.

In making their accusations, the Omagh unionists put themselves in a very false position. They were living at ease in their own homes, enjoying immunity from recruitment (largely because of opposition to it from Éire's government) and their "war effort" was limited to verbosities and military exercises. Bill, in contrast, was not only a war veteran but had also volunteered for a second time and was sacrificing his home comforts in support of the war effort.

Bill reacted with outrage and fury. His natural pugnacity was aroused. He went after the authors of the indictment. He carried his indignation home. A copy of the ludicrous dossier was lodged in one of his pockets where he could reach it, glare at it and snort over it whenever so inclined. Far from rushing to defend himself – in fact the army was not taking the allegations seriously – he pressed to have everyone who had had hand, act or part in bringing them be investigated, exposed and made to suffer for his wrong-headedness. He demanded that he himself be court-martialled, an action that would draw the accusers out into the open but also cause red faces among the army hierarchy. There were too many more urgent, less sensitive matters in hand and the dossier was dismissed as the trivial malice that it was.

In spring 1944, before D-Day, some American officers came to Bill in near-panic. A Very Senior Officer was coming to address a high-level assembly of American officers in Northern Ireland. They had found a hall

GENERAL DWIGHT D. EISENHOWER IN BELFAST, 18th MAY 1944.

where the address could take place, but it had neither stage nor any of the fittings and equipment needed – microphones, speakers, projectors, even appropriate seating. They tried using their own resources, but they were now way behind schedule: could Bill help? They either revealed to him, or somehow he soon realised, that the Very Senior Officer was the

Uncle Bill's Tin Hat

Supreme Commander Allied Forces in Europe, one General Dwight D. Eisenhower, here to brief his troops on the coming invasion.

Bill rose to the challenge enthusiastically. The Americans afterwards admitted to being deeply impressed by the way the appropriate skills and supplies had been sourced and the smooth sequencing of one group of specialists after another, largely civilian contractors, and the unflustered efficiency with which their assignments were completed. In short, the room was ready when Ike arrived. He briefed his officers who, three weeks later, were fighting on the Normandy beaches. The camps suddenly emptied, turning overnight from bustling settlements to deserted encampments.

After the war the Americans awarded Bill their Bronze Star Medal. In the photograph of his row of medals it is the one at the far right end. The citation referred to his services to the joint American/ British war effort

BILL'S MEDALS: THE MILITARY CROSS IS FAR LEFT AND THE AMERICAN BRONZE STAR FAR RIGHT.

over several years, but he himself felt that it was the "Ike episode" that had earned it for him. If he had not already acquired the trust and respect of the Americans, of course, they would not have brought their problem to him.

It was well after the end of the war, when he was living in Wimbledon, that a crested envelope arrived in the post one morning for Bill. It was from the American embassy in London informing him of his award of the Bronze Star Medal of the US Army. He was invited to the Embassy for a presentation ceremony and to bring two guests for the occasion. Christina and Michael (co-author of this book) attended. Citations were read out before each man received his award and it was surprising – startling even

CITATION FOR THE MEDAL OF FREEDOM

Lieutenant Colonel W. P. Andrews, British Army, performed services of exceptional value to the 8th Infantry Division from December 1943 to June 1944 at Omagh, North Ireland. His efficient supervision and maintenance of all billets and buildings occupied by American troops as well as his efforts to establish and maintain increased training facilities greatly aided the combat training of the division. Colonel Andrews' services were a material contribution to joint British-American cooperation in the common war effort.

BILL'S CITATION FOR THE UNITED STATES BRONZE STAR MEDAL.

– to hear what other men had done to win the bronze star; citations described very perilous, daring feats in battle. One involved an enemy tank being immobilised by the recipient. This was obviously not a medal created to acknowledge service that was merely meritorious. It was an important award for outstanding performance, albeit, in Bill's case, not in the face of the enemy.

His full row of medals illustrates that these have more serious functions than to brighten up the appearance of a drab uniform. They convey a good deal of information about the wearer to those who are familiar with them. Those at the two ends (Military Cross and Bronze Star Medal) are "Decorations" as opposed to the others, which are campaign medals. Decorations bespeak the quality of the man's performance. The other medals are more basic; they show the locations and the campaigns in which he has served; that his military career spanned from 1915 to 1945; that this man has seen "active service" in battle; and that he was an early volunteer in World War I – not a conscript. None of the medals, however, relates to his service in Mespot in World War I, no medal was struck to commemorate it. It was a notable campaign but one that history, and the medal-strikers, neglected.

It was left to the Americans to recognise his contribution in World War II: the British Army gave him only the standard campaign medal while the Americans awarded him the Bronze Star to acknowledge the value of his service.

The Americans left finally in 1944, just after Eisenhower's visit, and suddenly Bill found the camps once again empty and quiet. Then on 6th June came the abrupt realisation of where they had gone: this was D-Day, the invasion of the Normandy beaches, and the start of another phase of war in northern France. Many of the men from the camps of Tyrone ended up as bodies on the beaches or casualties in the hospital ships. The survivors pushed on to help conquer Nazi Europe.

But the camps were not left empty for long: their next occupants were Germans! The major war effort in Europe was now taking large numbers of prisoners, so the camps came to be used for Prisoners of War. The prisoners were not desperate to escape, happy to wait out the rest of the war in safety. They did not object to undertaking work outside the POW camps. Some were employed on building projects where Bill became responsible for them, some on farms. They used to march under a nominal escort to their work and once their routines were established it was not unusual to hear them sing as they marched. Singing was a standard practice in the Wehrmacht; during army basic training, one of the regular commands was "Sing!" The sound of their marching songs competed with the familiar birdsong along Tyrone's country roads.

BILL IN HIS LIEUTENANT-COLONEL'S UNIFORM, 1940.

A more chilling tone is struck by an incident after some Belgian army units occupied one of Bill's camps, and German POWs were to be sent to it on building work. Bill saw nothing untoward about this, but someone pointed out to him that the German occupation of Belgium had left relations between the two nationalities very bitter. Bill was alarmed and called another meeting with the Belgian commander, who did not speak

World War II

much English. Bill explained in plain language that these prisoners were under his control and he wanted them treated in accordance with the Geneva Convention. The Belgian didn't seem to understand him. Simplifying, Bill said "These prisoners: you must not injure them; you must not kill them." Understanding dawned on the other's face. He accepted this instruction absolutely literally. "No, Colonel," he said very seriously, "We will not kill them." Something in the way he said it left Bill shaken. At home that night, uncharacteristically, he several times repeated that reply of the Belgian's, "We will not kill them, Colonel," as if he were trying to wipe from his mind the horror suggested by its tone. In the event, the work party suffered no harm.

V-E DAY 1945.

There is no doubt that Bill worked extremely hard in those war years, 1941-45. He had a zest for the work and found real enjoyment in the opportunity to deploy his natural ingenuity, spontaneity and innovation with authority and freedom of action. His family have good recollections of his attitude to the work, even though it meant that he could give less attention to family life than before. He left Christina to manage the household, which she took on with vigour, growing vegetables, keeping chickens and turkeys in her garden and exploiting the underground cross-border food trade to supplement wartime rations. With Joan, Paul and John now off at boarding school in Dublin, Michael, aged 11, went to the Christian Brothers school in Omagh which Bill had attended in his time and found the freedom to infiltrate the wartime camps around the house.

Towards the end of the war Bill met up with a surgeon from Belfast who took an interest in his lung disease and thought that there might be some treatment he could provide. He persuaded Bill to allow him to take a peek at the lung and maybe a sample of tissue, just a minor procedure taking an hour or two in hospital. Christina was waiting for him to come home to Omagh that evening when she was called to the phone to be told that Bill was doing "as well as could be expected". She was on the first train in the morning and found him laid up in bed, immobilised and traumatised by what the surgeon had done. While probing he had penetrated the lung wall and caused it to collapse. The pain was, in Bill's words, "excruciating" and it was a life-threatening emergency. They managed to get the lung to reinflate so he could at least breathe, although it caused him great pain and effort. He recovered slowly and was discharged from the hospital, never to return to that place again.

On the 7th of May 1945, Hitler was dead and the German armies surrendered unconditionally in Berlin. The next day was celebrated as VE day for Victory in Europe as the Pacific war against Japan was still continuing. Bill stayed on in Omagh and, not long before leaving the army, had the pleasure of hosting the wedding of his one daughter, Joan, to a young civil engineer named Anthony Murphy whom she had met in Dublin. This was the first wedding in Omagh Church for over a year and brought out the whole town to view the event.

BILL AND CHRISTINA WITH THEIR DAUGHTER JOAN AND HER FUTURE HUSBAND, ANTHONY MURPHY.

BILL (FAR RIGHT) AT HIS DAUGHTER'S WEDDING IN 1945 SPOTS A FEW UNIFORMS AND TAKES COMMAND.

Bill did the organising: caterers took over the kitchens at Lissanelly; a big car was hired for the wedding morning and petrol cadged from everywhere despite the rationing restrictions. Gold lamé material for the bride's dress was sourced from one of the chaplains, apparently diverted from ecclesiastical couture, and a dressmaker was instructed by Christina on the style and design of the gown. The big church in the centre of Omagh was the chosen venue, but this caused a problem as the parish church for Lissanelly was the small church in Killyclogher, two miles outside town. This was where Bill and Christina had been married, and it was here that the wedding should have taken place in the eyes of the Catholic Church. Bill took aside the parish priest and persuaded him on the venue. However, his parish had missed out on the donation that was its right and so had to be compensated and Michael, aged 13, was despatched on his bicycle to Killyclogher with an envelope of pound notes for the parish priest.

So it was that, in keeping with Bill's and Christina's lifestyle, the wedding was celebrated with some panache at the impressive Catholic church in Omagh Town. The Bishop of the diocese, Dr Farren, based in Derry, travelled to Omagh to perform the ceremony. The wedding breakfast went on all day at Lissanelly and in the evening Joan tossed her bouquet from the roof of the front porch and the couple departed for their honeymoon in Bundoran. The bouquet was caught by the bridegroom's sister, Margaret, who was about the only female in the company who remained unmarried all her life.

THE WEDDING RECEPTION FOR JOAN ANDREWS AND ANTHONY MURPHY, LISSANELLY, OMAGH. BILL IS FAR LEFT.

After demobilisation from the army, and before starting work elsewhere, Bill went through a period of exhaustion and lassitude. He consulted a doctor who found him healthy and suggested the term "re-action" for his condition. The sufferer had not lost his sense of humour and for a while enjoyed quoting "re-action" as an excuse for anything and everything and spent a few weeks in pampered idleness while he regained his vim.

Soon he found a job to go to, a job in Dublin moreover, where his newly married daughter, Joan, as well as his four sisters, lived. Paul, his eldest son, was now studying for the priesthood in a seminary near Dublin where the strict regime didn't allow him outside the seminary walls, even for his sister's wedding, and gave him only two family visits per year.

The job in Dublin did not go according to plan, however; Bill's military methods (with the emphasis on innovation and improvisation, and the low priority given to cost) were not easy to adapt to a contractor's priorities in building runways at Dublin Airport. He left that job while there was still time to exercise his right to "reclaim" his pre-war job in London.

That entitlement to reclaim a job one had left to join the forces was a wartime enactment. There was a time limit on it, but Bill's entitlement was still valid even after his year working in Dublin. Whether his old firm would have welcomed him back anyway he didn't know. In the situation where he had volunteered to leave the job for the army at the start of the war and then had chosen to go elsewhere when the war ended, it was certainly a happier option to have a statutory right to the job than to have to go cap-in-hand to ask for it. Whatever the underlying feeling may have been, they welcomed him back and restored him to his former position in civilian life.

BILL AND HIS SON JOHN BACK TO CIVILIAN LIFE AFTER THE WAR.

CHAPTER 8

The Time of his Life

The war years had changed Bill's personal life beyond recognition. Children grow older and develop whether the world is at peace or at war. Now he and Christina had only the remains of a family – the eldest two of his children had left home and were no longer dependent.

TO THE BALL IN LONDON, EARLY 1950s.

The London to which he returned in 1946 had changed dramatically and not for the better. The housing shortage was the first, most pressing, concern, the result of the bombing and the fact that no house building had taken place for the five-year duration of the war. Rent restriction was in force to prevent exploitation and this had the effect of making people very reluctant to leave a property for which they had obtained a tenancy – such

A PEA-SOUPER IN LONDON 1952.

leases were at a premium – and house owners did not have the same incentive to let their properties. The Andrews family would have to be satisfied with much more modest accommodation than before the war. Bill concentrated his search on Wimbledon. Although there was only one school-goer left in the family, the fact that there was a good school there that the two elder brothers had attended was helpful. He still knew a lot of people in Wimbledon, family friends. After several months' arduous searching he was delighted to "get his hands on" a two-bedroomed flat in Wimbledon: even if it was in a different part of the borough – one not quite so "leafy" – it was close to the collocated school and church and the All English Tennis Club grounds. John, their second son, had now started his medical studies in Dublin and stayed with his sister and her husband and child, coming to London for the vacations only.

BILL AND FRIEND IN FORMAL MORNING WEAR, LONDON 1953.

The Time of his Life

IN UNIFORM ONCE AGAIN, BILL STANDING BEHIND CHRISTINA.

The changes to London were not, by any means, confined to the housing market. The middle-class school was now a Grammar School as defined by the 1944 Education Act, always associated with the name Ernest Bevin. This meant that it was free and, being government-subsidised, had altered its pupil catchment from fee-affording applicants to those allocated to it by a selection process based on the "eleven-plus" exam. A special arrangement applied for Catholic and other "religious" schools to be allocated pupils of their own religion. The selection process

ON AN ENGINEERS' TRIP TO BELGIUM, 1953: BILL IS FRONT LEFT.

had become part of the local authorities' functions, in this case Surrey County Council. Bill's skills in making arrangements stood up to the test of getting his youngest son admitted without having taken the Eleven Plus – he'd been in Dublin for the year when he became age-eligible to take it.

Bill lived in "digs" in London when he returned to his job there until The Flat was found and secured, his family left behind in Dublin. Christina and Michael then joined him and a new sojourn in Wimbledon began. It lasted, for Bill, 11 years until he retired in 1957 at the customary age of 65.

It started well. His employer, the Cement and Concrete Association, welcomed him back into its fold. A sufficient number of employees had stayed put to keep it running. Even though its peacetime function would hardly have existed during the war, some work had been found for the

AT THE CEMENT AND CONCRETE RESEARCH ESTABLISHMENT.

remaining staff and it still occupied the same offices in Victoria, Central London. It too was changing, however. A refreshing, if inexperienced, batch of new staff was recruited, mostly young – and bright in every sense of the word. This included a new director. Bill, not lacking in self-confidence, applied for that post even though applications were not publicly advertised and the post was filled by what amounted to an early

THE HIGH LIFE IN LONDON IN THE 1950s.

example of head-hunting. The bar was set high. Bill's application may have been cursorily acknowledged, but that was as far as it progressed. The eventual appointee (he played a walk-on part through the rest of Bill's professional life) was notable. His name was Sir Francis Meynell, a poet, book designer and publishing executive who had been an advisor to the Board of Trade in one of the war cabinets – many such appointees were not politicians. This Ministry that he was appointed to had as its nickname, the Ministry of Pots, Pans and Perambulators, and one of his jobs was to design utility furniture for wartime use. It had a very visible significance during the war and its head had been an effective organiser and not just a place-filler. His eminence must have been an emollient to the wounded *amour-propre* of the less famous rival applicant.

In 1948 Sir Francis paid a visit to the United States, and chose to be accompanied by his erstwhile rival, to the latter's great delight. It was a compliment and an opportunity he was more than pleased to accept. It was much more of an adventure, more of an experience, than it would be counted today. Transatlantic flights did exist, but they were not for those who liked comfort and, to an incomparably greater extent than today, carried real risk. Sir Francis and his companion travelled First Class on the *Queen Mary*. It was a sumptuous way to travel. Bill, though by no means a sybarite, luxuriated in it. The journeys through the States – taking in both Chicago and California – were by train. Stories of conversation in and viewing from the club car were brought back home to Wimbledon, as well as gifts for wife and son. It was an early high point of his eleven postwar years in London. His friendly relationship with the American officers he met in the North of Ireland was part of the reason for his having been invited to go. The presentation to him of his Bronze Star Medal in the American Embassy in London in '46 or '47 had become known "around the office". Before they set out he had contacted some of the Americans he had met during the war and arranged to meet them on his travels. Sir Francis wrote a report on his visit after they returned and touched on the question of anti-British prejudice in America: "The fact that it was clear to the eye, and even more so to the ear, that Col Andrews was from Ireland proved an asset in this regard."

Sir Francis had introductions to many influential Americans. In Chicago they met the newspaper magnate Robert McCormick, who seems to have read Bill's name and rank as indicating Old British Buffer. On their first meeting he opened with "I'll have you know, Colonel, that my mother's name was Murphy." "Mr McCormick," came the reply, "I'll have you know my daughter's name is Murphy." Relationships improved thereafter. It was quick and it was apt. Doddering old buffer he wasn't.

ON BOARD THE *QUEEN MARY*.

WITH FRIENDS IN THE GARDEN.

Bill's job was the promotion of cement and concrete as building materials. He travelled around the country addressing meetings and speaking with Local Authority officials to give information and technical advice on the uses of the products. In road-building, concrete was seen as a patriotic material as it was produced in the country and supported local labour and business, whereas bitumen for roads was an imported product. However, concrete roads were more complicated to design and construct and were often reserved for special locations such as steep gradients or areas needing hardwearing finishes. The association had a research facility in Wrexham Springs, Slough and Bill was often seen here testing and trying out new methods.

He published a number of pamphlets on concrete construction and was active in setting out standards for specification of concrete. Even so, the eleven years' remaining service leading to retirement were not the happiest or most successful of his life, pale by comparison with his war years, but certainly they were not all doom and gloom.

Bill made a return trip to Buckingham Palace. Through the Irish Embassy in London, he and Christina were invited for the annual garden party there. This was, of course, irresistible as a social occasion, although it proved to be something less than a memorable one. On this visit he had no encounter with the current reigning monarch, the present queen, but at least he was offered the best tea and buns that Lyons, the caterers, could provide, more than her grandfather had laid on at the award of the Military Cross.

On one occasion during the Cold War, a Russian Engineer was, for some reason, visiting England and was being looked after by Bill's firm, the Cement & Concrete Association. The firm was anxious that he should receive good impressions. Bill met him only when they brought him out for a little dinner party at a smart London restaurant on the night before he left. Shortly after the meal started he noticed some mild consternation around the guest. He realised that it was to do with the drink being served with the course. The Russian tasted it, replaced it on the table and showed no further interest. His hosts tried a different sherry, white wine, red wine. None of them evoked the slightest interest. Bill intervened. He suggested in English, of course, to the hosts that the Russian might prefer whiskey. They were put out. They'd been selecting choicest wines to match each course meticulously. "Really, Andrews! Whiskey with this delicate hor d'..." "DAAA ! VEESKEY !" Was the Russian's declared preference. A full bottle was settled at his elbow, geniality restored.

Every few years, throughout his life from 1940 onwards, health prob-

THE HIGH LIFE, THIS TIME IN DUBLIN.

lems with his lungs recurred. In Wimbledon, after the war, he developed a racking and persistent cough.

In 1957 lung specialists in London advised that an operation on one of his lungs was necessary. This was to remove cysts which had grown inside it and were occupying the space required to expand and draw in air with each breath. The surgery to remove them was done in one of the famous London hospitals. He was very weak following it. He gasped for air and the struggle strained his heart. He did recover, though, and returned to work for his last months before retirement. The office treated him with sympathy and consideration and he, in turn, still put in his day's work to the end. Before he left he had taken part in the interviewing and selection of his successor, as Head of Roads Division.

He left in good standing and, with Christina, retired from Wimbledon to a spacious, though somewhat cold, period house which they rented in Greystones, Co Wicklow in what was now, in another change of title, the Republic of Ireland.

GREYSTONES, 1960.

He hit the Republic with some éclat and obtained a short professional assignment from the Irish government which helped to ease his transition into the idleness of retirement. What was most impressive about this was that he was briefed in person for it by Seán Lemass.

Seán Lemass was to be the next Taoiseach, but he was then Tánaiste and minister of a department, possibly Local Government. The assignment he gave Bill was to visit the county engineers of the country and explain the advantages, both economic and physical, of using concrete in roads. The job didn't sound challenging (except, perhaps, that it would involve a good deal of travel) but the fact that Lemass, arguably the second most influential politician in the country, had briefed him on it in person was some indication of the respect he engendered at the beginning of his retirement. He had never met Lemass before and he was impressed by him, more so than he had expected to be. They got on well. Following that last task, his career as a civil engineer came to an end.

In Greystones, a genteel seaside village at that time, also a holiday

BILL IN RETIREMENT WITH HIS WIFE, TWO SONS, DAUGHTER, SON-IN-LAW AND GRANDSON. SERENDIPITOUSLY, BOTH AUTHORS OF THIS BOOK ARE IN THE PHOTO, MICHAEL, CENTRE BACK AND VINTY (VINCENT) ON HIS MOTHER'S KNEE.

resort, Bill became a prominent resident. There was a golf club in the village, but Bill, who had played off-and-on throughout his life, joined the one in Delgany a few miles away. I enquired casually why he didn't join the nearer one and the answer took me aback. The Greystones golf club did not admit Catholics to membership! Greystones was one of the Genteel Ghettoes of Protestants in the Republic of Ireland. In a country that was criticised for the excessive influence of the Catholic Church in its affairs, it was instructive to see this relic extant from the almost-buried past. Bill's family had holidayed in the village for many years and liked it, but had not picked up this vibration.

A great pleasure for him and Christina during his short retirement was the ordination to the priesthood of their eldest son, Paul.

Today Greystones has become much larger. It is now a dormitory town for Dublin with greatly improved rail service to facilitate commuters. A sports club was started about that time (this was in the years 1958 to 1960), which catered for tennis at first, extending to rugby later. It appears that this was not at all sectarian in nature because Bill was invited to chair the committee that was working to get it off the ground.

Retirement fell into a routine with a morning walk to ten o'clock Mass and to buy the daily newspaper, followed, in the afternoon, by a gin-and-

IT (Italian vermouth) shared with Christina. They settled well into the community, playing bridge and following the sporting and social life of the village. They were visited by their sons and by Joan, their daughter, whose husband Anthony was an engineer with whom Bill found he had a lot in common. Joan brought along her children, soon numbering six, their full complement of grandchildren at the time. Bill's sisters were celebrated doyens of Dublin society: they seldom strayed out as far as Greystones but kept in touch.

It should have been the case that he would have had a decade or more of relaxed retirement to close his eventful life. But this was to be no prolonged idyll. The damage done to Bill's health in the trenches forty years earlier recurred inexorably. The second lung was now congested with cysts and surgery was the only treatment to ease his breathing. Without it his difficulty in breathing would continue to grow worse and that was a death sentence. He was pessimistic about the outcome of further surgery. He had been near death after the first operation in London. His heart had been affected and his survival had been in doubt. Now his heart and he were five years older. The same post-operative strain would be inflicted again. He knew the risks – only too well – but decided to face up to them and agreed to the operation. The outcome was almost inevitable.

Fr. Paul Andrews, Bill's eldest son, takes up the story:

> In mid-October he underwent an operation on his lungs in the Richmond Hospital, and was put into intensive care. Mother and Joan and I went in to see him every day. He looked dreadful, and had a tracheotomy to ease his breathing, with the result that he could not speak properly. I cannot recall much of those three weeks between the operation and his death on 10th November 1960, at the age of 68. He could recognise and respond to us visitors. On one visit he whispered to me: I am proud of you, Paul. I treasured the remark.
>
> In those visits we were in the old dilemma of pretending that he was getting better while our eyes told us he was sinking. I was with him on the afternoon of 9th November. Going out the door I said: I'll see you tomorrow. He shook his head. I lingered, questioning his answer. He could not speak but with his right hand he pointed up, to heaven. That was his last communication with me, and he was right. He died during the night.

It was in the early hours of 10th November 1960 that Bill passed away.

The hospital phoned Fr. Paul and Joan and Anthony to tell them and they collected Christina and gave her the dreaded news. They then went through the sad routine of viewing Bill's body and formally confirming his identity. Christina was distraught and unbelieving: he had been her lifelong support and she depended upon him at times such as this, but he was gone.

BILL ANDREWS.

Bill was buried in Greystones at the Redford cemetery overlooking the sea on the road up to Bray Head. It was thirty years before he was joined by his wife, Christina, although they were quite close in age; his siblings, both brothers and sisters, lived to be much older than he – his life span was certainly curtailed by comparison with theirs. There can be no question: the pleurisy that he contracted in the trenches cut short his life soon after he had reached the age of retirement, but this truncation may be looked upon as the price he paid for survival. Had he not escaped from the charnel house of trench warfare, it is more than likely that he would have lost his life before the war was over. That was the fate of so many of his compatriots, war being no respecter of personal worth or talent or the degree to which they were prized by parents, siblings, wives, lovers or people who just appreciated them and knew their worth.

This is the account of just one life, which was preserved by the most fickle of chances. Had the lump of shrapnel been an inch or two lower, or the helmet tilted a half an inch higher or not fastened tightly, he would have lost that life. This story has set out to offer just one example of the potential which was randomly wiped out or grudgingly spared. Bill had a good life, a fruitful and a useful one, a life denied to so many in that slaughter, so many wonderful, talented young men, so many millions of them.

ACKNOWLEDGEMENTS:

Our main task in writing this book was to extract memories, both conscious and subconscious, from the hidden depths of our relatives' and our own minds. For decades the memories had lurked and faded, hidden in mental crannies and camouflaged by layers of later living. Some were lured out into the open by simple questioning, some raised doubts and suspicions and had to be gently prised from the crannies.

It astonished us how the appropriate stimulus would spark a hidden memory to life, and how difficult it was to find that one word or sound or picture that would evoke the response. We are wholeheartedly grateful for the generous help of all our relatives and friends in this work, the time spent over photographs and letters or just in idle but vital chat.

In particular we thank Joan Murphy and Paul Andrews, Bill's daughter and son. We are most grateful to the Omagh relatives, especially Bernadette McAleer, Christina's niece, who gave us whole-hearted and utterly invaluable help on each of our numerous visits to Omagh. We are most grateful to her and to the Kilkenny branch of the clan and the émigrés to Canada and America.

Special mention goes to Edwin Handcock, our forensic expert, Eugene Boyle and Eugene Brophy; Mary Andrews, Rachel and Sophie McCarroll; Emmet, William and Philip Andrews; Chris, Jay, Oliver and Della Murphy; Ciarán, Cliodhna and Aoife Murphy; Mairead Kennedy; Joe Fallon; Clare and Colm Lynch; Martina Goggin for her help in self-publishing; Liam O'Connor, Lisa Cunningham and Deirdre O'Neill.

LIST OF ILLUSTRATIONS:

PAGE

1	Bill's helmet.	Photo by Image Masters Photography Studio, Gorey, Co. Wexford, Ireland.
3	Strule river.	Authors' family collection.
4	Gateway to Omagh Gaol.	Photo by Vinty Murphy.
5	Governor's House, Omagh.	Photo by Vinty Murphy.
6	Treadmill building.	Photo by Vinty Murphy.
7	Omagh Town 1901.	Authors' family collection.
8	Bill and sisters, 1904.	Authors' family collection.
9	Boer pith helmets.	
10	Cork City Gaol gateway.	By kind permission of Cork City Gaol Heritage Centre.
12	Christina and Kathleen, 1897.	Authors' family collection.
13	Campsie Bar, 1903.	Authors' family collection.
15	High Street, Omagh.	Authors' family collection.
16	Cork City Gaol interior.	By kind permission of Cork City Gaol Heritage Centre.
17	Gaol Governor's Office.	By kind permission of Cork City Gaol Heritage Centre.
19	University College Cork.	
20	The Andrews family.	Authors' family collection.
22	King Edward VII's funeral.	
23	Bill's Student Registration.	By kind permission of University College, Cork.
25	Suffragettes.	
26	Punch cartoon.	From Punch archive.
27	Bill's family without him.	Authors' family collection.
28	German Feldkanone 96.	With thanks to Arie Dijkhuis.
30	French Adrian helmet.	Photograph by Rama, Wikimedia Commons, CeCILL, Cc-by-sa-2.0-fr.
31	Soviet Adrian helmet. Bill's Brodie helmet.	Authors' family collection.
32	Recruitment poster.	
33	Anti-recruitment poster.	
34	Newly-commissioned Bill.	Authors' family collection.
36	The warhorse on parade.	
37	The horse at war.	
39	Contalmaison Village.	An image from Google Earth under the fair use provisions of the Copyright Act.
40	Contalmaison Manor House before.	By August Dürler.
	Contalmaison Manor House after.	By kind permission of National Library of Scotland.
41	Church at Contalmaison.	Photo by Vinty Murphy.
42	Contalmaison field map. The depression at Fricourt.	
43	The battlefield.	Photograph by William Ivor Castle.
44	German machine-gun crew.	
45	Entrenched British troops.	

LIST OF ILLUSTRATIONS:

PAGE

46	Field map around Contalmaison.	
47	Orders of the day, 10th July 1916.	By kind permission of The National Archives, Kew.
48	Awaiting the order in the trench.	
49	Field sketch of machine-gun emplacement.	By kind permission of The National Archives, Kew.
50	Newspaper report.	
51	Bill's own helmet.	Photo by Image Masters Photography Studio, Gorey, Co. Wexford, Ireland.
52	The moment of truth.	
53	Map Contalmaison trench layout.	Map by Michael Andrews and Vinty Murphy.
54	Contalmaison village after the battle.	
55	Shrapnel shell.	Drawing by Vinty Murphy.
56	German machine-gun emplacement.	Photo by Vinty Murphy.
57	Helmet detail.	Photo by Image Masters Photography Studio, Gorey, Co. Wexford, Ireland.
58	Helmet detail.	Photo by Image Masters Photography Studio, Gorey, Co. Wexford, Ireland.
59	War Diary extract.	By kind permission of The National Archives, Kew.
61	Bill's military cross.	Photo by Vinty Murphy.
62	George V presenting awards.	
63	Buckingham Palace.	Photograph by Petr Kratochvil reproduced, with thanks, by Public Domain Licence.
64	The London crowd, 1917.	
65	Troops playing football, 1917.	
66	Lunchtime, 1917.	
67	Bill's medal card.	By kind permission of The National Archives, Kew.
69	Map of Mesopotamia, 1918.	Map by Michael Andrews and Vinty Murphy.
70	Troops in Mesopotamia.	
71	Casualties in Mesopotamia.	
72	Warship in the Shatt-al-Arab.	
73	Mounted soldiers in Mespot.	
74	Bill with fellow new-arrivals.	Authors' family collection.
	Bill with fellow officers.	Authors' family collection.
75	River transport, Mesopotamia.	
76	British troops enter Baghdad.	
77	A village in Mespot.	
78	Basra, 1918.	
79	The officers in Mespot.	Authors' family collection.
81	British Army Crossley lorry, 1918.	
82	Bill in 1922.	Authors' family collection.
84	Christina McAleer, 1922.	Authors' family collection.
86	Bill and Christina.	Authors' family collection.

LIST OF ILLUSTRATIONS:

PAGE

87	Wedding Photo, 1924.	Authors' family collection.
88	Christina and Bill on their wedding day.	Authors' family collection.
89	Bill's father's death certificate.	By kind permission of the Irish Registry of Births, Marriages and Deaths.
90	The growing family.	Authors' family collection.
91	Bill with his Austin car.	Authors' family collection.
92	Car on holiday.	Authors' family collection.
93	Bill at Armentières.	Authors' family collection.
94	Another family car.	Authors' family collection.
95	Wimbledon 1938.	
96	Engineers at Sans Souci, Potsdam.	Authors' family collection.
97	Lunch at Autobahn Labour Camp.	Authors' family collection. *We apologise to anyone upset or distressed by the swastika in the background: we decided it was too much a part of the switches and ironies of Bill's life story to omit.*
	The autobahn.	Authors' family collection.
99	A bomber over London.	
100	Children evacuated from London. The London blitz.	
101	The Brodie helmet gets a new use.	
102	London 1940. The blitz.	
103	Belfast 1940.	
105	Bill sketched by Joan, aged 15, 1941.	By kind permission of Joan Murphy.
106	Strule View.	Photo by Vinty Murphy.
107	Lissanelly.	Photo by Vinty Murphy.
108	Bill's 4 children during WWII.	Authors' family collection.
109	Christina and children in the hay.	Authors' family collection.
110	Building a Nissen hut.	
111	A Nissen hut encampment.	
112	American army chaplains.	Authors' family collection.
113	A standard Nissen hut.	
114	The chapel in a Nissen hut.	Authors' family collection.
115	Post-war publicity for the "chapel".	Authors' family collection.
116	B-specials.	
117	General Dwight D. Eisenhower.	
118	Bill's medals.	Photo by Vinty Murphy.
119	Citation for the U.S. Bronze Star.	Authors' family collection.
120	Bill in uniform, 1940.	Authors' family collection.
121	V-E day, 1945.	
122	Bill, Christina, Joan and Anthony.	Authors' family collection.
123	Bill at his daughter's wedding.	Authors' family collection.
124	Joan's wedding photograph.	Authors' family collection.

LIST OF ILLUSTRATIONS:

PAGE
125	Bill and his son, John.	Authors' family collection.
127	To the ball in London, early 1950s.	Authors' family collection.
128	A pea-souper London, 1952.	
	Bill and friend in morning wear.	Authors' family collection.
129	In uniform once again.	Authors' family collection.
	On an engineers' trip to Belgium.	Authors' family collection.
130	At the CaCA research establishment.	
131	The high life in London in the 1950s.	Authors' family collection.
132	On board the Queen Mary.	Authors' family collection.
133	With friends in the garden.	Authors' family collection.
134	The high life, Dublin.	Authors' family collection.
135	Greystones, 1960.	
136	Bill in retirement with family.	Authors' family collection.
138	Bill Andrews.	Authors' family collection.

Cover Photo: Photo by Vinty Murphy and Michael Andrews. Tunic by kind permission of Irish Military War Museum, Collon, Co. Meath.